How To Get It Together When Your World Is Coming Apart

How To Get It Together When Your World Is Coming Apart

DONALD W. MORGAN

Fleming H. Revell
Old Tappan, New Jersey

Unless otherwise identified, Scripture quotations in this publication are from The New King James Version of the Bible. Copyright © 1979, 1980, 1982 Thomas Nelson, Inc., Publishers.

Verses marked TLB are taken from The Living Bible, Copyright © 1971 by Tyndale House Publishers, Wheaton, Ill. Used by permission.

Scripture quotations identified MOFFATT are from THE BIBLE: A NEW TRANSLATION by James Moffatt. Copyright 1926 by Harper & Row, Publishers, Inc. renewed 1954 by James A. R. Moffatt. Reprinted by permission of the publishers.

Scripture quotations identified AMPLIFIED are from the Amplified New Testament © The Lockman Foundation 1954–1958, and are used by permission.

Scripture quotations identified PHILLIPS are from THE NEW TESTAMENT IN MODERN ENGLISH, Revised Edition—J. B. Phillips, translator. © J. B. Phillips 1958, 1960, 1972. Used by permission of Macmillan Publishing Co., Inc.

"The Road Not Taken," Copyright 1916 by Holt, Rinehart and Winston, Inc. and renewed 1944 by Robert Frost. Reprinted from THE POETRY OF ROBERT FROST edited by Edward Connery Lathem, by permission of Henry Holt and Company, Inc.

Acknowledgments continued on page 192.

Library of Congress Cataloging-in-Publication Data
Morgan, Donald W. (Donald Walker). Date
    How to get it together when your world is coming apart / Donald
W. Morgan
        p.   CM.
    ISBN 0-8007-1599-3
    1. Christian life—1960–   2. Consolation.   3. Morgan, Donald W.
(Donald Walker). Date   I. Title.
    BV4501.2.M5842   1988
    248.8'6—dc 19   88-11317
                                                              CIP

Copyright © 1988 by Donald W. Morgan
Published by the Fleming H. Revell Company
Old Tappan, New Jersey 07675
Printed in the United States of America

CONTENTS

FOREWORD

WE TEND TO think of sin only in terms of the Ten Commandments—thou shalt not kill, lie, steal, or commit adultery. But sin comes in many shapes and forms and, in my opinion, one of the more reprehensible ones is making the Good News of the Gospel boring and dull. Whether you are a preacher, teacher, writer, or simply a witness, to make the proclamation of the Christian message dull or pedantic or esoteric borders on the unforgivable. It is like turning wine to water.

That is one reason why I so appreciate my friend, Don Morgan, as both a preacher and a writer. He brings great enthusiasm, freshness, and urgency in communicating life-changing truths. I have, in the past, been a guest preacher in two churches that he has pastored, one in Cleveland, Ohio, and the other in Wethersfield, Connecticut. I found both parishes warm and lively, brimful of enthusiastic lay ministers who were partners with Don in outreach and mission. Such a congregation, it seems to me, is the result of expounding simple but too-seldom-heard truths with excitement and authority, undergirded by sound biblical application.

In this book, Don deals with the relevance of the faith in Jesus Christ for those whose world is coming apart. All of us have in major or minor ways come to that point. Even as I write this foreword, I've probably never had more seemingly insoluble problems in my life, both personal and those related to the church I serve. I used to feel guilty about having such problems. Surely my world would not be coming apart if I were a person of greater faith, ability, or wisdom. I'm coming to understand that authentic faith does not protect the believer from those times of crisis. Indeed, our faith gives us the resources to deal with them.

I have always had a fondness for a good adventure yarn. My vacation reading invariably includes some book of that genre. I thoroughly enjoyed the "Indiana Jones" movies and couldn't wait to see how he would finally win out over snakes and crocodiles, pygmies and thugs. Lately it has occurred to me that I have the opportunity to enjoy my own predicament, rather than vicariously enjoy someone else's. If and when my present problems are solved, I will come across new ones. To have faith is to believe that God is in the situation with us and will make rich compost out of the worthless garbage of our lives.

I recommend this book to every Christian who understands that life is always going to be made up of snags and obstacles where we feel things are falling apart. Don Morgan fleshes out some of those situations for us and outlines our options in those dark times. In his words, we can "take cover" in all sorts of unhealthy ways or we can "discover" our values, ourselves, and our God and His purposes, and from there we can *recover.*

How to Get It Together When Your World Is Coming Apart is written in clear and pithy prose, buttressed by many personal experiences of the author and other people. The book is illuminated by gleanings from the minds of poets, writers, and theologians over the ages. It is a veritable gold mine for every serious Christian prospector who would discover for his or her own life just how good the Good News is.

BRUCE LARSON

ONE

WHEN YOUR WORLD IS COMING APART

A TELEPHONE CALL came to me late in the morning one day. It was from a company executive. One of his truck drivers, a man in his forties, had had a heart attack and died instantly. He had been married little more than a year, and he and his wife had a baby son. Would I go and break the news to this woman that her husband, who had left the house that morning apparently well, was now dead? Of course I would. It was a dreadful task, but someone had to do it.

I recall finding their home, the second floor of a two-family dwelling. She was not a member of my church. She did not know me; I did not know her. I recall that her baby, *their* baby, lay in a crib nearby. I thought about that now fatherless child who lay there so quietly and innocently. This poor child would never know his father. As sensitively as I could, I identified myself and indicated I had unhappy news. Then I gently began to relate the events of the morning. At last, having paced it all very carefully, I disclosed to the woman that her husband was dead. Her face congealed with shock, even terror, and then a quiet wailing came forth. Suddenly this woman who had finally achieved a happy marriage and had her own little baby to care for felt her world coming apart!

I know the feeling. I've known it for years. I experienced the same when I was a boy of thirteen. It was Sunday, just one week before Mother's Day. We were dressing for church—my father, my brothers, and I. My mother was in the hospital, recovering from surgery that had taken place earlier that week. Things had gone well. She was expected home in a few days. In fact, the day before, I had visited her in the hospital and found her looking radiant. I planned to see her later that day and take flowers for which I had been saving money.

The phone rang. Somebody answered. At the moment, I was standing in front of the mirror in my room, combing my hair. I had just plopped a delicious dark brown chocolate in my mouth and was feeling rather good. It was a beautiful spring day, the first day of May, and I was young and happy about life. But just then, I heard my aunt call up to my father. "It's the hospital," she stated, with a tone of voice that was intended to be neither alarming nor casual. "They want us to come over right away." Somehow I knew what it meant. There was no doubt in my mind: My mother was dead! I learned later that she had died from an embolism quite unexpectedly. But at that moment up in my room, I suddenly felt sick at the pit of my stomach. I rushed to the window, lifted the screen, pushed my head out, and let the chocolate fall out of my mouth to the ground below. I didn't want that chocolate anymore. My world was coming apart!

You and I both know these experiences are not unique. Most of us—perhaps all of us—have those times when life puts us through the worst.

There was once an excited little girl who rushed into her kindergarten class one morning and announced: "My mother just had a new baby and it was born too soon, so they put it in a percolator!"

Life can put us in a percolator. Sooner or later, we confront a moment when life comes to a halt, time is frozen, and a momentous event takes place—a devastating loss, a traumatic development, a massive and deep rupture in life. Like Job, we ask: "My God, why? Why this? Why me? Why now? Why at all?" We've been going along, taking things for granted, when suddenly our world is coming apart.

It's like being thrown into a tailspin. We're airborne, flying high, climbing upwards, when all at once the ship lurches and plunges earthward in a spin! Everything is out of control. Everything is swirling around us. We scarcely know where we are. How can we bring the plane out of the spin? How can we get it together, when our world is coming apart?

There are three possible responses we might make. It's good for us to think about these responses so that we can see which is the best response to make. That way, we can keep on top of things and learn to manage our lives for the best.

For one thing, we can *take cover*. That's how many react to trauma in their lives. They close their eyes, close their minds, close their hearts. They react as children might when frightened in bed at night, pulling the covers up over their heads and hoping whatever it is will go away. But that's escape! That's running from life. That's refusing to face reality and to deal with it positively.

There are varieties of escapes. Resignation is one—simply giving up. Hedonism is another—losing ourselves in pleasure or losing ourselves through drugs and alcohol. We only get ourselves in deeper. We risk losing all control over life. Denial is yet another form of taking cover. We deny that whatever it is that has happened to us has in fact happened. We can also develop unlovely qualities of harshness and bitterness. We grow hardened, grim, bitter, and self-pitying. We become singularly unpleasant to have around.

So, in one of several ways, our response when life is coming apart may be to take cover. "It is too easy," wrote Teilhard de Chardin, the priest-paleontologist who had such a clear, vast vision of life, "to find excuses for inaction. . . . This is defeatism. . . . Defeatism is invariably unhealthy and impotent."

But if we refuse to take cover, if we decide this is no way to deal with life, **we can *discover!*** We can turn our lives into an era of discovery. We can become explorers of our world and of life and of ourselves! We can experience the meaning of God's words in Hosea: "I will . . . make the dale of Trouble a door of hope" (Hosea 2:15 MOFFATT). We can discover!

We can discover life's true values. Maybe we need this experience to come to our senses, sort out our priorities, learn what life is all about. Let things go along without trials, without tribulations, and we have a way of getting fat with ease and shallow with good times. We devote ourselves and our energies to the wrong things and find satisfaction in the wrong ways. But when our world is coming apart, we can discover life's true values. An anonymous writer put it this way:

> When wealth is lost, nothing is lost;
> When health is lost, something is lost;
> When character is lost, all is lost.

We can discover our true strengths. We can discover things about ourselves, good and beautiful things, that maybe we didn't know we possessed.

I recall how after we went to the hospital and got the heartbreaking news that our mother, a good and faithful and beautiful woman just turned forty, was gone, we returned home. My father, my two brothers five and eight years my senior, and I gathered in a huddle in the dining room. As we stood there with our arms around one another, crying our hearts out, my older brother, then in college, said, "Now we'll see what we're made of!" To this day, those words stand out as some of the most important words I have ever heard. When life comes apart, we have a lifetime opportunity to discover our inner qualities, our true strengths—"what we're made of" as my perceptive older brother put it—to let them come forth and allow them to grow!

We can discover ourselves. When hard things happen and we are put to the test, we can come to know who we are, who God made us to be, those special and distinctive things that shape this something called *self*. "If you know yourself and know your enemy," goes a wise, old Chinese adage, "in a hundred battles you will win a hundred times." The greatest crisis of life is an identity crisis, discovering who you are!

We can discover God. We can discover who made us, who gave us life, who gave us all we love, who is the Source of our being and the Goal of our striving, without whom at the center of our lives and the highest priority of our living, nothing finally comes out right. We can discover God, not as a remote and philosophical belief to which we occasionally and reverently tip our hats, but as a present Reality and a constant Help.

"I had known what it was to believe in God," was the

entry of the mother of Josiah Royce in her diary one night after facing a great danger while crossing the continent in a covered wagon, "but now He came so near that I no longer simply believed in Him but knew His presence there. . . .That calm strength, that certainty of One near and all-sufficient, hushed and cheered me."

"Oh, these people are born scared, live scared, and die scared," said the great Albert Schweitzer, who brought medical and spiritual help to the people of Africa. "I limit myself to preaching to them that in spite of all appearances to the contrary, behind all the seeming mystery and cruelty of life, there is not terror but love, the Father of Jesus Christ."

We can discover God, and that is the pivotal, central discovery of a lifetime! And once we have discovered God, we can discover God's purposes for us. He has them. I am convinced of this. I *became* convinced. God did not squander all this talent and ability, all these fantastic possibilities for nothing! Why should He invest so much in our lives if He had no purpose, no plan? When we find that purpose and discover His plan for us, then our lives can be fulfilled and we can begin to move, really move! That is the meaning of those exciting words of Romans 8:28: "And we know that all things work together for good to those who love God, to those who are the called according to His purpose."

And we can discover the infinite riches of life fulfilled, of life ablaze with beautiful, mind-blowing possibilities. This discovery may not come all at once. It may not come for some time. It may not, in fact, come for years. But it will surely come, in God's time! If we, *discover* rather than *take cover*, then "the valley of weeping," promises Psalms 84:6, will become "a place of springs."

Defeat may serve as well as victory
To shake the soul and let the glory out.
When the great oak is straining in the wind,
The boughs drink in new beauty, and the trunk
Sends down a deeper root on the windward side.
Only the soul that knows the mighty grief
Can know the mighty rapture. Sorrows come
To stretch out spaces in the heart for joy.

EDWIN MARKHAM

Did you hear that? "Only the soul that knows the mighty grief can know the mighty rapture." If, rather than take cover, we discover—discover life's true values, discover our true strengths, discover ourselves, discover our God, and discover His plan for us—then **we can _recover!_** We can move on, with our lives finding a new form, taking a new shape, so that the black coal becomes the stunning diamond—a treasure! We can move on to new and greater glory, new and greater happiness. We can recover!

And all the jarring notes of life
Seem blending in a psalm,
And all the angles of its strife
Slow rounding into calm.
And so the shadows fall apart,
And so the west winds play;
And all the windows of my heart
I open to the day.

From _The Gates of New Life_
BY JAMES S. STEWART

TWO

GOD'S HEALING FOR LIFE'S HURTS

IT WAS MANY years ago, but I still remember her. I never knew her name. I never knew where she lived. I really knew very little about her. Let me simply call her "the woman on the left side of the trolley car."

I was a college student at the time, attending Tufts College (as it was called then, before it became a university), commuting daily from my home in Lexington, Massachusetts. Each day I would take a bus to Arlington Heights, and there I would change to a trolley car. Often, as I got on the trolley car, I would notice a woman, perhaps in her forties, sitting on the left side. Always she sat with her head turned away as though she were looking out the window, even when there was nothing much to see out there.

I began to wonder about that woman. Why did she sit there, unfailingly on the left side? Why was she always looking out the window? Then one day I happened to catch a glimpse of her face and then I knew. On the left side of the woman's face was a very large, very dark birthmark. That's why she was always turned away from the other passengers, her fellow humanity. No one must see her face! No one must see her birthmark!

Then I thought, *What a thing to live with!* How much of her life is affected by this? For how many years has she planned and plotted to sit or stand in just the right place so that others could not see? For how many years has she expended enormous effort concealing her secret? What interior effect has it had upon her? Upon her every move? Upon her relationship with people? Upon her self-image, her sense of self-worth? This was the great hurt of that woman's life. I felt for her, I really did. To this day, I remember her only as "the woman on the left side of the trolley car."

But now, think about this: How many people in this world have *secret* hurts? How many have *secret* pains? Not a birthmark, nothing external, but something internal, something within—in the heart, in the mind, in the soul— a secret hurt that has affected them for years!

Let's bring this closer to home: What of *our* hurts, yours and mine, and what of God's healing? We all have hurts. I know I do, and I dare say you do. What are you harboring in the secret recesses of your soul; what great sorrow, what lifelong disappointment or frustration, what deep and abiding hurt? And what of God's healing?

Jesus had hurts. We know this from many passages of Scripture relating to His life. He was "a man of sorrows and acquainted with grief," according to the "suffering servant" reference from Isaiah 53:3. Very likely one of the greatest hurts our Lord experienced came early in His ministry, when He returned to His hometown of Naza- reth. Here He was, a local boy making good, but what kind of reception did He get? Luke 4 describes it. Naturally the townspeople were interested in what He had to say. They had heard extraordinary accounts of His accomplishments elsewhere. They invited Him to say a few words at the synagogue service. But when He finished reading the Scripture passage, He made comments that upset them and aroused their wrath and hostility. They rose up and, seizing Him, hustled Him out of the synagogue to the edge of town near a high cliff. This was a lynch mob! They intended to push Him over the cliff to His death, these dear folk of Nazareth! He, however, maintained His composure. He didn't get rattled. He didn't lose His head. It has always amazed me how Jesus handled the situation. He walked calmly, resolutely, through the crowd and "went His way." But be sure of this: It hurt! Boy, did it hurt! It must have grieved Him to be rejected by the very people He had known and loved. So even in the life of Jesus, our Lord and Savior, we are led to the issue of life's hurts and God's healing.

But now have you noticed that in the nature of things, healing is part of the process of life? It's as though God planned it that way. God, in His infinite wisdom, planned for healing. When a branch is cut from a tree, in the course of time, a sticky substance oozes out, covers the gash, solidifies, and new bark slowly forms across the exposed place. If you happen to cut your hand, blood spurts out, providing instant cleansing, washing away the impurities. Then that same blood miraculously congeals, clots, and gradually hardens into a tough protective cover. Eventually new skin appears and healing has happened. Why can't our cars heal themselves like that—heal their own dents, nicks, and scratches? Someone could make a fortune producing self-healing, self-repairing automobiles!

We may lose someone in death. All at once it happens,

a loss so devastating that our world is in a swirl. At first the pain is almost more than we can bear. We become obsessed with the thought of the loss. The reality of it hangs over us like a dark, dark cloud that never seems to go away. That's what I experienced when I lost my mother. That's what that woman experienced when she lost her husband and had to face loneliness and the prospect of bringing up her child without her husband. But in the normal course of events, the pain subsides, the loss becomes less oppressive, and we begin to pick up the pieces and live again. It's called "grief work." It's part of God's plan. This, you see, is the healing side of God who wants to help us with our hurts and who sent One for the express purpose "to heal the brokenhearted" (Luke 4:18).

What, then, do we do? How do we handle life's hurts—the rejection of someone dearly loved, the misunderstanding of someone deeply admired, the loss of someone greatly needed? How do we cope and get it back together and move on with life? How do we begin the normal, natural process God has provided?

The first thing we need always to do is to *acknowledge the hurt.* We need to recognize it. We need to admit it's happened. I'm not speaking here of little hurts, incidental slights which we should never allow to occupy our time and attention. I'm speaking of the great hurts which, if left unattended, can eat away at our inner lives and warp us. This is no time for repression of our hurt. This is the time for exposure, the time for saying, "Yes, it's happened. It's true. I feel the pain. I feel the loss. Oh, God, how I feel it!"

When I lost my mother, my conscious mind registered the loss, but my subconscious mind did not want to accept it. How do I know this? I dreamed about her. There was one dream in particular that gave it away. I dreamed I was approaching a large hospital with walls around it. It was more like a fortress when I think about it. I knew my mother was in there. She was alive—only people weren't telling me. They were keeping the truth from me; they were keeping *her* from me! Then I would awaken and realize she was really dead. Still, given half a chance, my mind refused to accept her death.

A woman came to talk to me one day. She had been experiencing symptoms which were difficult to decipher. Her doctors were uncertain as to their meaning. The longer she and I talked, the more I felt there was something hidden there that was at the root of her trouble—a great hurt, a painful loss, unexpressed, perhaps even unacknowledged. "Tell me about your mother," I inquired, working a hunch, and she began to talk about her mother who had died several years before. Suddenly she was convulsed in tears and implored, "Why did my mother never love me?" She proceeded to pour out a long list of examples of the tragic rejection she had endured. It was a sad tale. She herself was astonished by what she was saying, for she had never faced the rejection in this way. Still, the dike was broken and the healing could begin.

We need to acknowledge our hurts and sorrows. We may need the help of someone—a counselor, a minister, a friend. But we need to get it out, see it for what it is, expose the wound, and allow the healing light of day to come in!

The second thing we must do is to *accept it and allow forgiveness to wash the impurities away.* It's happened. That cannot be changed. It's had an impact. That cannot be altered. Now accept it, and realize that what is needed at this juncture is forgiveness, the most therapeutic reality in the world!

Can you forgive the one who has done this to you? Can you forgive life itself that has imposed this upon you? Can you forgive God that He allowed this to happen—even though perhaps for some reason that for the present escapes your understanding? And can you forgive yourself insofar as you were part of the reason, part of the cause, part of the picture which resulted in this intense pain or loss or hurt?

"Is there a balm in Gilead, to heal the sin-sick soul?" I don't know about you, but the relevance of that song, that plea, haunts me! I have come to know that, through Christ, God has made provision for healing through the power of acceptance and forgiveness. That is an important truth, the most important in all the world. Because it is true and because we let the reality of it flow in and through us by faith, then every hurt can be healed, every sorrow can be assuaged, every tragedy can be overcome. So we come to accept it and we allow forgiveness to wash away the impurities.

The next thing we need to do is to **walk close to Him.** As an act of faith, we draw near to God; we draw near to Christ. Rather than withdraw, which would only compound our difficulties and our sorrow, we walk with Jesus. We tell Him how we feel. We tell Him what we've experienced. We tell Him how deep is the pain, how painful is the hurt, how hurting is the anguish. And we ask Him to show us how to use it constructively, positively; how to "make the dale of trouble a door of hope."

It has been scientifically proven that we can bear pain better when we share it with another. We can endure injury and hardship better when we experience companionship in our suffering, somebody who is going through it with us. There may be another human being who can do this with us and for us, and that will help. But this I also know: There is One, "a man of sorrows and acquainted with grief" (Isaiah 53:3), who knows all about it and who came "to heal the brokenhearted." He says, "Come to Me, all you who labor and are heavy laden, and I will give you rest" (Matthew 11:28). Ours is the only faith in the world that provides this kind of companionship! Ours is the only faith in the world where God Himself shares it all! Remember the hymn:

> I come to the garden alone,
> While the dew is still on the roses,
> And the voice I hear, falling on my ear,
> The Son of God discloses.

> And He walks with me and He talks with me,
> And He tells me I am His own,
> And the joy we share as we tarry there,
> None other has ever known.

You want to handle life's hurts? You want to know God's healing? Then walk close to Him, walk close to Jesus.

The fourth thing we need to do is to **turn the hurts into an Alleluia!** We convert the weakness into a strength. We convert the loss into a gain. We convert the injury into a blessing, not only for ourselves but for others.

Max Cleland, secretary of state of Georgia, came out of the Vietnam War minus both legs and one arm. He could have given up. He could have grown bitter, angry, cynical—gnarled and consumed with self-pity. But what good would that have done? That would have only turned one negative into more negatives, an avalanche of them! No, he sought positive ways to use his life, and he has described the results in his book, *Strong in the Broken Places*.

Boy, I like that title! What a thought! The places on our bodies which have been broken can become the strongest places. The places in our hearts which have been broken can become our places of strength, understanding, compassion, wisdom, and love. It's the alchemy of faith! "Only the soul that knows the mighty grief can know the mighty rapture."

How would you react if you learned your beautiful teenage daughter had just been in a motorcycle accident and was going to lose her leg? That was the grim news that came to my friends Robert and Arvella Schuller several years ago. At the time they were in Korea, where Dr. Schuller was to address a large gathering of ministers and church leaders. Then came the sickening call! At once they headed home. They wanted to be at their daughter Carol's side. But what grief, what sorrow, they felt!

Flying over the Pacific, Dr. Schuller felt tears welling up in his eyes. Not wanting to make a scene in that public place, he bolted to the lavatory, shut the door, locked it, and wept loudly and profusely. "Bawled" is the way he put it. Then the thought came to him from God: "Schuller, if you have to bawl, turn it into a ball! Praise God while you cry." Remembering how a short time earlier his Korean friends had sung "Alleluia," he began to cry out: "Alleluia, Al-le-lu-ia!" As he put it, he turned his "tears into pearls of praise!"

We can do that! We really can! We can take the hurts of life and turn them into our strengths. We can take the sorrows of life and turn them into gains of understanding, service, and faith!

That's what Joni Eareckson Tada did. That beautiful young woman was involved in a swimming accident as a teenager. She sustained fractures at the fourth and fifth cervical levels of her spinal column and became permanently paralyzed from the neck down. What she went through was horrendous, but she did it! Refusing to give up, she fought back. She found new ways to be creative.

She became in many ways a new person. She experienced in a beautiful way the love and power of God, and she has become an inspiration to millions. She turned her hurt into an Alleluia with Christ's help!

We can do that, too! We may not be able to avoid the hurts of life. ". . . You do not know what a day may bring forth," we are advised in Proverbs 27:1. We have no assurance tragedies will never come our way. Many of us have already experienced deep sorrows and staggering losses. But there is something more, and this is our winning edge. We have One who was "a man of sorrows and acquainted with grief," who came "to heal the brokenhearted." That's all we need. The healing love and miraculous power of Jesus Christ! With Him, whatever the hurt, we can turn it into an Alleluia.

THREE

THE SIGN
IN THE SKY

ONE AFTERNOON SEVERAL summers ago, the storm clouds gathered at our mountainside farm in Vermont. The day darkened and the rain fell. We were just returning from a drive and as I got out of my car, I noticed some people on the opposite side of the dirt road that runs in front of our house. They had stopped their car near the bank which overlooks the lower field and gives a spacious view of the valley below and the mountains beyond. These people standing there were looking intently at something in the sky. So, of course, we looked, too. There it was—a rainbow! It was the clearest, fullest, brightest rainbow I had ever seen—so spectacular and awesome that I could hardly believe my eyes!

Then, wanting to capture the glorious sight, I ran into the house, grabbed my camera, and ran out. Almost immediately I snapped the shutter. However, it was not soon enough, for in those few moments the rainbow had faded and was gone. Never, as long as I live, will I forget it. Always will I retain in my memory that vision of beauty. I've seen the setting a thousand times—that field, those woods, the gorgeous valley below, the mountains beyond. God willing, I shall view it a thousand times more. But as long as I live, I shall never forget the loveliness of that one beautiful rainbow.

Still enthralled by the vision of the rainbow, I remembered the scriptural account of Noah and the Flood when God so despaired of humanity He thought to wipe out the human race and start over. But, the account tells us, God became sorrowful and repented of what He had done. He regretted the destruction and devastation, and, with the sign of the rainbow, He assured Noah that never again would He destroy the human race with a flood. From then on, God and humanity would be bound by a contract, a covenant of mercy and love. God said, "I set My rainbow in the cloud, and it shall be for the sign of the covenant between Me and the earth" (Genesis 9:13). That was God's promise. That was His pledge. I remembered this passage after seeing the magnificent rainbow. I remembered the rainbow was His sign in the sky, the sign of God's love and grace.

Years ago, Dr. H. H. Farmer commented on the apparent inability of many people to retain a sense of God's presence and power around them. He said, "If it is true that the beauty of tree and flower, of birdsong and sunshine, is the free bounty of God, it is strange that these people should be entirely unaware of it, as indeed most of them are. If only God would, so to say, sign some of His gifts. If only, like the artist, He would put His signature at the foot of some masterpiece of colouring in the sky."

But, in a sense, God *has* done that. Remember God's pledge to Noah recorded in Genesis: "I set My rainbow in the cloud, and it shall be for the sign of the covenant between Me and the earth." So, the rainbow becomes a kind of signature—God's signature—God's reminder of His everlasting mercy and love.

Now, what we need to see, first of all, is **how much you and I require such a sign** or **signature from God.** We need those visions, those bright and revelatory moments, when the truth of an ultimate hope comes through and reassures us of God's love. We surely need them, and the remembrance of them, when our lives are badly shaken. Winston Churchill once raised the question, "What would become of us if God wearied of mankind?" My heavens! What a thought! Yet, what would we say? How do we respond? When things get bleak, are we tempted to entertain such an idea of God walking out on us? When our world is coming apart, are we tempted to conclude it's a Godforsaken world, after all?

A while ago, a friend of many years wrote me a letter laced, I sensed, with latent despair. Normally a hopeful person, he sounded surprisingly sad, even melancholic. He admitted to being "almost overwhelmed by the forces that appear to have done in the Christians" around him. I found myself asking: *What's happening to my friend? Is he losing faith? Is he himself being "done in," as he put it?* He seemed to have raised in his own way the chilling question of Winston Churchill about the possible abandonment by God of His people: "What . . . if God wearied of mankind?"

When the chilling thought strikes us, we might remember that for centuries there have been those who said (almost gleefully) that God had long since deserted us. They were called *Deists* long ago. More recently, twenty years ago in fact, it was the "death-of-God" people who raised the grim spectre of the possibility that after God created the world, He left it to spin endlessly toward its fate. God was some sort of clockmaker who, having made the clock and wound it up, had left it to go on ticking by itself. However, movements proposing these cynical notions don't last long, as most people don't resonate to their point of view and their bleak conclusions. Something in us cries out for a loving, caring God. Something in us recoils at the suggestion that He has abandoned us. We need these signs in the sky, and we need to believe what they tell us.

For consider, in the second place, *how despairing of life we would be without these signs.* Succumb to the giant of despair and we're soon in a bad way. Thomas Aquinas, that brilliant intellect who a thousand years ago had deep thoughts about God, identified despair as "the deadliest of all sins." A good case can be made for the claim. Let us suppose we never saw a rainbow, never heard of one, never knew of one—and hence did not know what it signifies in God's scheme of things. We would presently and surely succumb to the most devastating despair and, yes, incapacitation. We would, in fact, suffer a triple loss.

1. We would suffer a loss of strength. Growing paralysis would take over. A kind of spiritual rigor mortis would set in. We would experience a loss of power to deal with life.

2. We would suffer a loss of will. We would have declining drive, diminishing motivation, decelerating incentive. There would be nothing to lead us on, hold us up, propel us forward.

3. We would suffer a loss of hope. No bright vision would inspire us, no lofty dreams precede us. We would soon wallow in dark and deadly cynicism. We would be in a bad way!

All this would bedevil us if we did not have the word

straight out of faith experience and God's Word: "I set My rainbow in the cloud. . . ." Notice: in the *cloud!* Not in the bright sunlight, but in the cloud! In the darker moments of life, His sign is nonetheless there.

And yet, and this is our third point, **Scripture is persistent in this hopeful and reassuring message.** I remember someone saying to me, "When in doubt, consult the Bible." I should add, "When in despair, turn to the Word of God." You could hardly do better. Review God's assurances. Rehearse God's promises. Saturate yourself in the faith literature that has inspired great men and women for centuries and brought them through difficult times equal to, if not far exceeding, anything that might come our way. Throughout God's Word there is this declaration: God is faithful. He will not let us down!

In the prophetic book of Hosea, God says, "I will not execute the fierceness of My anger . . . for I am God, and not man" (Hosea 11:9). In the book of Micah, it is said, "Who is a God like You, pardoning iniquity . . . ?" (Micah 7:18.) In Isaiah, there is the timely reminder, pointedly responding to Churchill's foreboding, "Have you not known? Have you not heard? The everlasting God, the Lord, the Creator of the ends of the earth, neither faints nor is weary" (Isaiah 40:28). Later, the Apostle Paul, never one to be daunted, reaffirms the theme, declaring that while "we are perplexed," we are "not in despair" (2 Corinthians 4:8). And, yes, just as the first book of the Bible cites the rainbow and its message of God's steadfast love, so the last book gives a vision of the heavenly kingdom, and discloses, "And there was a rainbow around the throne" (Revelation 4:3). It's as though God were to say, "Do you get it now? Do you finally get it?"

Writers of more recent times have not missed the point. George Matheson, in his much-loved hymn, "O Love,

That Wilt Not Let Me Go," coming out of his own struggles and anguish, wrote:

> I trace the rainbow through the rain,
> And feel the promise is not vain.
> That morn shall tearless be.

Wordsworth perpetuates the theme:

> My heart leaps up when I behold
>   a rainbow in the sky;
> So was it when my life began;
> So is it now I am a man
> So be it when I shall grow old,
>   Or let me die.

Do you know the delightful story told by Dick Van Dyke about a first-grade boy trying to impress his classmates? "When I grow up," he boasted, "I'm going to be a lion tamer. I'll have lots of fierce lions, and I'll walk in the cage and they'll roar." Then the tyke noted the incredulity registered on the faces of his fellow students, and quickly covered himself: "Of course," he added, "I'll have my mother with me."[1] To be sure, he'd better not count on it! But we have it from the Word of God that God will be with him. God will be with us in the thick of things. We have His word. We have His sign.

But now if this is true, notice, in the fourth place, what it means for you and me: Bring it home. Bring it right into your living room. Bring it right into your situation, when your world is coming apart and you're desperately trying to get it all together. At our weakest and most vulnerable moments, when things are most disheartening and discouraging, when viciousness and human depravity and tragic developments threaten to do us in, *we are nonethe-*

less confronted with a question, "Would you so easily give up?"

No sooner are we challenged than we are reminded, "God doesn't give up!" He doesn't give up on you and me; He doesn't even give up on the world. He's still trying. In Marc Connelly's play, *The Green Pastures*, the archangel Gabriel is the hothead always ready to blow his horn and call it a day for the world. Fed up with things, he importunes God to let him sound the trumpet, bring down the curtain, and get on with Judgment Day. But on one such occasion, God softly rebukes him, saying, "Gabriel, have you noticed that every now and then mankind turns out some pretty good specimens?"

They do come, those bright and shining moments. They do come, those beautiful and reassuring visions. They do come, the good and faithful folk who here and there brighten the landscape of life and give us an unforgettable sight of something better and finer. Never again is life the same. Never again does our valley look the same. God's Spirit and light have broken through into human experience, refracting into a brilliant and heartwarming array of colors. Ever after, we live in the glory of its afterglow and the reminder of its truth!

God doesn't give up! Why should you? He doesn't call it a day when clouds gather, but instead throws out a rainbow, and says, "Remember? Remember?"

The wife of Martin Luther—he called her "Kate"—took her husband to task one day (as wives sometimes do). Luther had allowed himself to become pessimistic and downcast. Finally, having had as much of it as she could take, Kate told her hubby off: "Come out of it, Martin! Come out of it! God isn't dead!" Isn't that what the rainbow vision tells us? "Come out of it, friend! Come out of it! God isn't dead!"

You're going through a difficult time? You're ready to call it quits? You're ready to surrender to despair? Hold on, now! No one is saying it's easy. No one is saying there won't be tough sledding ahead. What we are saying is, giving up is the worst thing you can do. That's a no-win situation if there ever was one. That really puts you out of the running! What I am saying is, there are signs, there are disclosures. They're beautiful and they're breathtaking. They come of a divine mercy and of a divine love that never let us go. Hang on to those signs! Hang on to them! Look up and not down; look to the sky! "I set My rainbow in the cloud." And then at the last, "there was a rainbow around the throne."

FOUR

IS GOD FOR REAL?

PEOPLE HAVE LOTS of questions about God, but none more compelling than this: Does God exist? Most of us, from time to time, have our share of uncertainties, even doubts, but never more surely than when life hits us hard and our world is coming apart. Then we really wonder. Then we really ask: "*What's* behind it all? *Who's* behind it all? Is *anything* behind it all?" So let's tackle this. Let's get back to basics on this, go back to square one, go back to the beginning—back to God! As we try to get it together, to build our lives on a sure footing, let's secure the foundation of faith and deal with the pestering, perennial question: Is God for real?

Now, I know as soon as we have said that, there's an issue we have to be up front about. It's this: Are we—you and I—going to be clearheaded and unbiased about this question of faith in God? You see, you may be making certain assumptions. You might know or assume me to be a man of faith, so then you just might wonder: *Can he get really beyond his professional belief and wrestle with a question like this? How seriously can somebody making his living in the ministry question the existence of God?* It's like the two Cockneys who passed by a London church one day. They happened to notice the outdoor bulletin board which carried the sermon topic for the following Sunday: "Is There a God?" The Cockneys stopped, read the sign, squinted at each other, and then one of them, with a twinkle in his eye, said to the other, "Wouldn't it be a caution if he said there ain't!"

So let me tell you something about myself. I have had a lifelong interest in these issues. Even more, I have had a lifelong intentionality about being tough-minded when it comes to something as basic as this. I have spent many years wrestling with these questions and trying to make sure I came up with solid answers. Believe me, I've been tough with myself!

In fact, in my search for a secure faith, I have gone through almost every point of view you could think of, including atheism. For a short time in my life, I was a "card-carrying" atheist. I really was—I actually denied the existence of God. I rejected Him outright. And I was quite sure in my own mind why soft-minded people believed in Him.

It happened this way: I was studying psychology at Tufts in pursuit of a bachelor of science degree. I was attending a seminar on advanced psychology when my crisis of faith came. We were discussing Gestalt psychology, as it was then understood, and reflecting on a series of dots on the blackboard. We noted how the mind tends to relate the dots, even though they are not necessarily related. We seem to visualize lines running through them, giving them a certain shape or form. In other words, the mind projects order and relationships where none exists.

This was a favorite demonstration of Gestalt psychology, always good fun to play around with.

Suddenly something clicked in my mind. "Maybe," I blurted out before my professors and classmates. "Maybe that's what we do when we profess belief in God! We project order out there in the universe where there is none. Our belief is nothing more than the projection or figment of our minds. Then we say, God must be behind it all. So we project God. That makes God imaginary, simply the projection of our minds. There is no order! There is no God!" I went home that night a convinced atheist!

I didn't sleep very well, however. I began to realize I had a new problem, a serious problem. I began to think— if the order out there which we think we see and which leads us to believe in God is unreal, imaginary, then our scientific research itself is finished, a waste of time. You can't do scientific study, reach certain conclusions, develop theories if there is no order—if the whole thing is topsy-turvy, sheer chaos with neither rhyme nor reason. For then all such study becomes pointless, an exercise in futility. You must believe in the order simply to be a scientist. You must assume it and never question it.

In the course of my sleepless night, I realized the whole thing was insane. I realized I must assume the existence of order and the rationality of things or surrender to total hopelessness. If only to be a scientist, if only to be productive and get the job done, I had to have that much faith! So then, to claim to be a scientist and to deny faith— or its necessity—is sheer nonsense! Since then, I have found the best scientists understand this.

The following day I returned to class, the next session of the seminar, ready to repent and to recant. I shared with my professors and classmates that my line of reasoning the day before was absurd. If I were so easily to dismiss God, I could as well dismiss science and we could all go home and twiddle our thumbs! Overnight, I recovered my faith in the cosmos and in God! That was the end of my short-lived, twenty-four-hour brush with atheism!

Of course, whether you're a believer or a nonbeliever, it's good to be able to back up your position. G. K. Chesterton once said something to the effect that the function of an open mind was like that of an open mouth: eventually to shut down on something solid. "Always be ready," says 1 Peter 3:15, "to give a defense to everyone who asks you a reason for the hope that is in you." If you're a believer, be ready to defend it. If you're a nonbeliever, be ready to defend that, too! Fair enough, wouldn't you say?

A Scottish clergyman, a canon, was traveling from Scotland to London by train. When the train stopped at Cambridge, a heavyset man of about forty got on and entered the same compartment. The new arrival was carrying a book, *Why I Am Not a Christian* by Bertrand Russell, which he opened, allowing the title to be plainly visible. The train started up, then stopped, and the conductor announced a ten-minute delay. The Scotsman looked at his watch and said audibly, "O dear, I may miss my connection."

"Let us pray you do not," said the man from Cambridge with a wink and an air of condescension.

"Pulling my leg a wee bit, are ye?" said the canon.

"I dare say," the man chuckled.

"Ye nae believe in prayer?"

"I do not!" responded the man.

"May I ask, what then is y'r faith?"

"I," said the man, "am an atheist—does that offend you?" The canon shrugged.

"Have y' then read much o' the Good Book?"

"Not a line since I was sixteen."

"Do y' know the arguments for faith by Saint Thomas Aquinas?"

"No," said the man, smiling.

"Have ye perhaps read Saint Augustine?"

"I never felt the need to," he said.

"P'haps Cardinal Newman? E'en Malcolm Muggeridge?"

"No, no. They all seem to me gasbags."

The Scottish clergyman studied the man thoughtfully. "Dare I be frank, sir, to a total stranger?"

"Of course you may, sir. I rather enjoy a healthy difference of opinion."

"Well, then, sir," rejoined the canon. "Ay have news f'r ye. Y're not an atheist. No, no. Y're an ignoramus."[2]

So, then, what are the classical arguments for belief in God? Some would call them proofs, proofs of God's existence. They're not proofs really, not in the strictest sense, but reasons for believing or, my preferred expression, intimations of Deity. There are four such classical arguments, and they represent the thought of some of the finest minds the world has ever known. The distillation of such thinking has resulted in these four arguments of why it is more reasonable to believe in God than not to believe in Him.

The first is called the *cosmological* argument. This means that we observe cause and effect relationships throughout creation. Every effect has a cause; everything is caused by something. So, we observe that even the universe, all of creation, must therefore have a cause— what Aristotle called the First Cause. That is God. We say it is logical to assume the cosmos had a cause or a beginning, which was God. Therefore, this is known as the cosmological argument.

The second argument for God is called the **teleological.** *Teleo* means purpose. It says there is purposefulness throughout creation. There is design. There is intentionality. Numberless processes clearly fulfill a purpose, and where there is purpose or intentionality, it is reasonable to assume there is mind or intelligence behind it.

I recall how one day many years ago when I was serving a church in Litchfield, Connecticut, I was preparing for confirmation class. I entered the classroom where the chairs had been arranged in a semicircle for the young people soon to arrive. Then I noticed at the center of one chair an upturned tack. *That's odd,* I thought. Then I happened to look at the other chairs. They, too—all of them!—had upturned tacks in the center. "Ah, hah!" thought I. "This has the makings of a plot. Somebody is up to something!" Clearly there was a manifest purpose for those tacks. They were arranged by a mind, albeit a scheming, mischievous mind!

So, too, with creation, the universe, and everything in it. From microcosm to macrocosm, there are systems, arrangements, patterns which suggest an Intelligence, the mind and reality of God. So when the great entomologist, Jean Henri Fabre, was asked if he believed in God, he responded, "No I don't *believe* in God; I *see* Him everywhere!" So, too, when the noted physicist, Lecomte de Nouy, felt awestruck by the evidence of God throughout creation, he wrote an award-winning book, *Human Destiny,* and declared that chance alone could not account for creation, but only God! This line of reasoning is called the teleological, that the purposefulness and design of creation are evidence of a Mind, a Designer, an Intelligence—God!

The third argument for belief in God is the **moral** or **ethical.** It is sometimes connected with philosopher Immanuel Kant's moral imperative concept. Basically, it asserts that every human being has some sort of moral or ethical sense. While its content may be taught or may be the result of conditioning, still the capacity for such concern is instinctive, part of our basic equipment. We are born with it. We are born with a capacity for moral concern.

Every human being, even the most perverse, feels a compelling need to justify himself, to show the rightness of his position. Even a small child evidences this, particularly when that child has been treated unfairly. Children seem to have a natural and incredibly keen sense of justice. They react to unfairness and quickly let you know about it! Philosophers and psychologists have reflected upon this inherent moral sense.

We ask, "Why?" Why indeed?—unless behind everything there is a Moral Being. Someone who cares about right and wrong, justice and injustice, decency and honor. The amazing pervasiveness of the moral imperative in human life logically leads to belief in God. This is called the moral argument and tomes have been written about it.

The fourth argument for God is called the **ontological.** How's that for a fancy word? Frankly, this argument is my favorite. I really go for this! The original work for this argument was done a thousand years ago by Saint Anselm, one of the greatest minds of all time. Periodically, others have come up with much the same theory, even though they might have thought they were doing something new. Still, the concept here is the hardest to communicate and to comprehend. Every so often I see it with great clarity, and then I just know it's true, and then it gets fuzzy again! It's like that rainbow seen from our mountain farmhouse—first you see it, then you don't.

Essentially, it goes like this: The *idea* of God is evidence of God! The mere fact that human beings can think about God suggests His reality. In fact, it compels the reality of God. It's like hunger: The very fact of hunger implies the existence of food. Why would we have hunger if there were no such thing as food to satisfy it? The same is true for sex. The very fact of sexual yearnings implies the possibility of sexual fulfillment. Every fundamental hunger has an answer. "I believe," said Anselm, "in order to understand." You could say, "I believe because all my being cries out for God, for the living God, and that without God, there is no ultimate fulfillment." Now, yes, this may be a bit difficult to understand, but I have come to find the ontological argument the most convincing. It brings to my mind the lines of a poem:

> Like tides on a crescent sea-beach,
>   When the moon is new and thin,
> Into our hearts high yearns
>   Come welling and surging in—
> Come from the mystic ocean,
>   Whose rim no foot has trod,
> Some of us call it Longing,
>   And others call it God.
>
> WILLIAM HERBERT CARRUTH

There are other arguments or cases that have been developed—many very convincing—for belief in God. But these are the classical ones. What they say is not that God's existence is proved beyond the shadow of a doubt; there is still room for faith, thank God! There is, in fact, very little anyone can literally *prove* about anything. All of us live more by faith than by fact. It is only an illusion that we do otherwise. However, these arguments, while not proofs, are highly compelling reasons why intelligent, reasonable, and brilliant people through the ages have concluded that God exists; they have believed the Grand Surmise!

But now, I must tell you something. The real issue is not what are the good reasons for belief. "The heart has its reasons which reason knows nothing of," said Pascal. *The real issue is your decision, your choice.* It comes to this: Do we choose to believe in God? Do we choose to risk yielding our lives in faith to Him?

You see, God made us free. He wanted us to be free, so that we could either profess Him or deny Him. He really wants us getting into this thing freely, because we want to, not because we must—not by the force of the obvious. It's like marriage. Who wants to have a shotgun marriage? Who wants to be forced into it because he or she (generally *he* in these circumstances) has no choice? No, a good marriage is where two people freely say, "I want to get into this because I believe in you and want to bet my life on you."

If you want proof first, you will wait forever. You will be lacking in the one essential for all good relationships— trust. God doesn't want our faith because we *must* believe; He wants it because we *want* to believe. He leaves enough uncertainty in the picture so that we are free to choose Him or to reject Him. So it's our choice; it's our decision.

At this point, we need to acknowledge some strong language in Scripture, Hebrews 11:1, 3: "Now faith is the substance of things hoped for, the evidence of things not seen. . . . By faith we understand that the worlds were framed by the word of God, so that the things which are seen were not made of things which are visible." Then the writer of Hebrews winds it up with this: "But without faith it is impossible to please Him, for he who comes to

God must believe that He is, and that He is a rewarder of those who diligently seek Him" (Hebrews 11:6). Of course! It's an act of trust. It's a choice! It's a decision!

Did you know psychologists have found that we are all naturally believers? We come into the world believing. Children are natural believers. Maybe that's why Jesus said, "Unless you . . . become as little children, you will by no means enter the kingdom of heaven" (Matthew 18:3). What happens is that we cease believing because of some trauma or profoundly disturbing event. Something happens. Maybe it's emotional or maybe it's intellectual. More often it's emotional. Then we decide, *I just won't believe in God.* Sometimes it's our way of getting back at God. Sometimes it's our way of asserting our superiority, our way of saying of ourselves, *There but for the grace of God goes God.* But it's a choice. It's a decision we make—and of course, that's the way free will works!

So, what it comes to is this: Do we want to believe in God? Do we want to confess that He exists? Do we want to be believers? The ball is in our court, where it's always been. God wants it there.

You see what a possibility this opens up? All we need do is say, "Yes, God, I do believe. I do affirm You with all my being. You do live, and because You live, You can live in my life and my life can be different. Praise God Almighty. He lives!"

FIVE

CAN WE KNOW GOD?

THERE LIVES IN our town a little four-year-old charmer whose name is Carrie. Her parents belong to the church that I serve as minister. They often bring her to the services and to the children's programs. One day, while Carrie was playing in her living room, our church service, which is regularly televised over the community channel, came on the TV screen. When I as the minister appeared on her TV, Carrie reacted noticeably. She seemed to know me, as well as the setting, the Meetinghouse of First Church. Her parents, who had been watching her with fascination, wondered if she really knew that this was her church. Testing her, they asked who that was on the screen. Quick as a flash, she answered, "God!" Just as quickly, her wonderfully affirming father answered, "You're close!"

Close? Maybe—if you want to stretch it a bit, but not close enough! Not close enough when it is God we want to know. What is God like? Isn't that what lots of people are wondering? What are His qualities, His traits, His characteristics? Nobody has seen God at any time—not even on television! How then can we know Him? The issue is important because how we see God determines how we see life. How we understand God becomes the filter or the lens through which we perceive life. Who or what we believe is behind it all affects how we feel about everything and what we see as life's possibilities. So let's deal with this question: *Can we know God?*

There's a story about a man who went to heaven and was soon fascinated by all the people he met. One person in particular caught his attention, someone who appeared to be a doctor. At least he wore a doctor's white coat. He carried a doctor's black bag. He had a stethoscope hanging around his neck. Moreover, this man seemed to be very important. Judging from the way the others treated him, he was a V.I.P.! So the newcomer asked the first person he could, "Who is that doctor over there?"

"Oh," came the reply with a chuckle, "that's not a doctor. That's God. He just likes to play doctor!"

Well, what is God like? Would you know Him if you saw Him—even if He were wearing a doctor's coat? Could you describe Him? Would you recognize Him?

Before we try to answer these questions, let's make a critical distinction. What do we mean by "knowing God?" What do we mean by having knowledge of God? It's not merely knowing *about* Him. That won't do; it isn't very fulfilling or satisfying. I can say I know Hawaii—that is, I know *about* Hawaii. I know it's out there somewhere in the Pacific Ocean. But that isn't the same as knowing Hawaii firsthand, really experiencing Hawaii. There's a world of difference between these two forms of *knowing*. I can say I know the coast of Maine. That is, I've seen pictures of it. I've seen maps showing its location. I've heard about it.

But until I've been there, until I've absorbed the roar of surging waves or tingled to the ocean spray upon my face or thrown my body into that refreshing, ice-cold salty surf, I'm a long way from knowing the coast of Maine!

Now, put this distinction in terms of people. We can know them or we can know *about* them. There's a difference. You see, you can't really know somebody unless you've known that person firsthand. You've got to see him or her at close range. You've got to observe the person in a variety of circumstances, how he or she reacts to this or that situation, and most of all, how he or she reacts to other people. You've got to spend time with another person to really know him or her.

I've gotten to know Billy Graham. Until a few years ago, I didn't know him, except as a familiar face on the television or in a newspaper. I might have had all kinds of impressions or opinions about him, but that's all they would have been: impressions, opinions. They could have been entirely wrong. Then I met Billy Graham when I chaired the Southern New England Billy Graham Crusade. So it came about that I got to know him personally. I met him for the first time when I and others picked him up at Bradley airport just outside Hartford. I took him to the hotel in the city. I visited with him in his hotel room. I had dinner with him and kept several appointments with him in different parts of the larger community. For an entire week, I sat with him night after night on the platform of the crusade in the Hartford Civic Center. Later I was with Dr. Graham in Sheffield, England, for Mission England. And yet another time I was with him in California on the final night of the Anaheim crusade. So, over a period of time, I got to know Billy Graham quite well, personally. I must say he is truly a rare and remarkable human being, extraordinarily gracious and faith-filled, well deserving of all the honor and respect accorded him worldwide these many years. He is without a doubt one of God's greatest evangelists of all time. But the point is: I certainly know him better today than I knew him previously via television or a newspaper or some other indirect way! Those exposures to this man allowed me only to know *about* him. Now I really know him! There's a world of difference!

Of course, I'll have to admit, people react differently to Dr. Graham. He has a story he likes to tell about himself. It seems he was staying at a certain hotel in the South. While he and a friend were going up in the elevator, another passenger spoke to Billy's friend, saying, "I understand Billy Graham is at this hotel!" "That's right," said Billy's friend, "and here he is, right beside you." The surprised man quickly turned and looked at Dr. Graham, and then said, "What an anticlimax!"

That wasn't as bad, however, as the time when Billy was making a commercial flight. A rather unpleasant drunk was sitting in front of him, causing a disturbance. The attendant had tried everything to quiet the man, without success. Becoming desperate, she finally said, "Sir, don't you realize that sitting directly behind you is the Reverend Doctor Billy Graham?" With that, the man climbed out of his seat, stumbled into the aisle, peered strangely at Dr. Graham, and announced with a carrying voice, "Why, Dr. Graham, you'll never know what you have done for my life!"

So the reviews, even for Billy Graham, are mixed! But you get the point: To really know somebody, it isn't enough merely to know *about* him or her. You need to experience that person firsthand.

And yet, knowing God isn't quite that simple, either. You see, knowing people isn't so difficult. After all, they are within creation; they are somewhere within the world. We can knock on their door or call them up on the phone. God is beyond creation, outside creation. If God is truly the Creator of all, He is above and beyond that which He created. He cannot be known simply by our rummaging around in His creation. It's like our knowing an artist or a composer: You can't find the artist inside his painting, nor can you find the composer within his musical composition. To be sure, you can surmise certain things about the painter or the composer from their creations, but they remain surmises. Somebody may get some idea of what you are like by what you have made, but they cannot know you except by meeting you face-to-face.

In the same way, we can surmise certain things about God by looking at His creation, but they remain surmises. There is only one way God can be known, and that is by His making Himself known. He must take the initiative and reveal Himself to us. If God wants His creatures to know Him (and if He is a God of love, surely He would want to), then He must find the way to project Himself into His creation. He must put Himself into the picture, so that we can get a glimpse of Him and see what He's like. Short of that, He remains a mystery; He remains *Deus Absconditus*, God Unknown. Short of divine revelation, God in His fullness cannot be known.

Now, here we come to the crux of the issue: Has God made Himself known? Has God taken those steps to reveal Himself to us, His children? The glorious answer is *yes!* God has done just that, and this is the central claim of the Christian faith. God broke through the barrier of time and space. He transcended all the walls that separate us. He made Himself known to us through Jesus Christ. It's what we call the Incarnation. It means "embodiment," the divine embodiment of God at the human level. "For in

Him," says Paul in Colossians 2:9, "dwells all the fullness of the Godhead bodily."

There is a point here that's absolutely necessary to understand. It lies at the heart of the issue of whether we can know God. If God who is Love wanted to relate to us personally, He would need to become personal. If He wanted to establish a self-revealing relationship with His human creatures, He would need to come among us in a form we could relate to, a human form. If He wanted to manifest qualities of love, tenderness, and mercy, as well as purposefulness, intentionality, and justice, He would need a vehicle capable of expressing these very qualities— a human life to relate to human beings. Always, in every sphere, knowledge moves from the known to the unknown. So, if we are to know Him, God would need to take form in what is best known and familiar and personal to us. It is the central claim of the Christian faith that God has done precisely that. "The Word became flesh and dwelt among us, and we beheld His glory" (John 1:14). Everything you and I need a God for can be found in Jesus Christ!

Do you see what this means for you and me as we try to sort out what we are, who we are, and where we are—as we try to get our lives together? Do you want to know what God is like? Come to Jesus. Do you want to know the mercy and love of God? Look to Jesus. Do you want the joy-filled experience of associating with God in a personal way? Walk with Jesus. Do you want all of God that you could ever find this side of heaven? Find it in Jesus. It's all there! Every bit of it! "He who has seen Me has seen the Father," said the Lord of Life (John 14:9). Paul put it this way: "The light of the knowledge of the glory of God [has shined] in the face of Jesus Christ" (2 Corinthians 4:6).

A small boy was looking longingly at a portrait of his

father who had been away at war for a long time. That boy missed his father dearly. It seemed so long since he had seen him. Would he ever see him again? Then the young lad said to his mother, "Oh, Mother. I do wish Father could step out of the frame." In Jesus Christ, God, our Father, has done precisely that. He has stepped out of the frame into our world, into our creation, into our lives where we can touch Him and know Him—in Jesus Christ!

You see what this means? What an exciting possibility it holds out? How that can be the very centerpiece of faith as you get your life together and prepare to deal with anything that might come along? You can know God! I can know God! You and I can know Him because God has made it possible through Jesus! So live in that light. It is so much brighter, so much happier. Live in that love. Live in that peace. Live with this intimate and all-fulfilling knowledge of God through Jesus!

SIX

DOES GOD KNOW YOUR NAME?

ONE OF Jack Benny's last appearances was on the "Tonight Show." He told Johnny Carson, "If God came to me and said, 'Jack'. . . ." Then Benny paused, letting that sink in, and added slowly, "You know, God knows practically everybody." But does He? Can He? How can we be sure?

A little girl in a church I served some years ago was overheard by her parents as she was reciting the Lord's Prayer. She gave it a new twist. "Our Father," she began, "who art in heaven." Then she said, *"How did you know my name?"* That was her understanding of the Lord's Prayer. In her innocent way, she raised an issue. Does God know her name? Or mine? Or yours? How personal is this God after all? How all-knowing?

A friend in the ministry many years ago was an instructor in religion at Amherst College. He gave a lecture one day on the teachings of Jesus. In the course of the lecture, he said that God "knows individuals, loves them, watches over them, tries to help them." After the class, he was approached by one of the more thoughtful students. This young man said to my friend, "Do you yourself believe that God is interested in individuals?" My friend answered unhesitatingly, "Yes!" The young man was silent for a moment, and then asked, "Do you think God knows my name?"

It's not hard to imagine why that young man raised the question. We live in an immense universe. Its boundaries are unknown. The scope of it boggles the mind. You and I are but microscopic entities in a vast expanse of space. Somebody once summed it up this way: "Astronomically speaking, Man is insignificant." Put that way, you really wonder: How well does God know us? How well *can* He know us?

There are really two towering questions here. Both have to be dealt with; both require an answer. Notice what they are. Here's the first: Are we important enough for God to know us? Here's the second: Is God great enough to know about us? That is, is it conceivable God's mind is so incredibly great that He can keep tabs on all of us?

So the issue is twofold: The one question having to do with our importance in the scheme of things, and the other having to do with God's greatness. People have tended to dismiss the issue on the basis of the one question or the other. Either they've said we're too insignificant for God to be bothered—He really has better things to do!—or they've said God cannot conceivably have such a mind as to know everything—it's too much even for God! Either way, it's a put-down! Either they put us human beings down or they put God down. Either they set limits on human beings or they set limits on God. So let's zero in on the questions and see how we can answer them.

Question Number One: **How important are you to God?** How important in the scheme of things is every individual, every human being? We can answer this in two ways: by looking at creation and the things which are apparent and obvious around us, and by looking at what Scripture tells us and particularly what Jesus tells us. Remember, we have established that for us, Jesus is the revelation of God. If we want to know what God is like, we look to Jesus. If we want to know the mind and character of God, we look to Jesus. Is there any other authority to whom we might turn? Clearly, the judgment of history is that Jesus, above all, is the source of divine knowledge.

As we look at creation, we see there is no known creature equal to, let alone greater than, man or woman for his or her incredible properties, capacities, and attributes. Of course, we can engage in all sorts of philosophical nonsense to dispute that. We can resort to idle speculation as to what may or may not exist elsewhere. But based on the evidence at hand, there is no other creature of such extraordinary qualities or capacities. We may be small in the scheme of things, but does size determine importance?

The psalmist made an observation twenty-five hundred years ago which has never been successfully challenged: "What is man that You are mindful of him, and the son of man that You visit him? For You have made him a little lower than the angels, and You have crowned him with glory and honor" (Psalms 8:4, 5). Shakespeare said much the same: "What a piece of work is man! How noble in reason! How infinite in faculty! In form, in moving, how express and admirable! In action, how like an angel! In apprehension, how like a god! The beauty of the world! The paragon of animals!"

In all the current scientific research concerning the beginning of the world and the origin of life, there is strong evidence confirming the marvel of human life, the uniqueness of human beings, and their conspicuously special place in the order of things. However creation came about, however God pulled it off, there is a unique role and destiny He has given us human beings. As for the quote "Astronomically speaking, Man is insignificant," somebody has wittily replied, "Astronomically speaking, Man is the astronomer!"

When we look at the Word of God and examine the teachings of Jesus, this belief is upheld. Throughout biblical history, God's dealings are with people—with *individuals*, in fact. Nowhere in the pages of Scripture do we get the picture of a philosophical God detached from human life, who is uninterested in human beings. To the contrary, He is a God who moves among us, cares about us, and makes the effort to relate to us. The Christian faith is unique in its emphasis upon the importance of the individual. In eastern religions, the individual becomes little more than a drop in the bucket, or more exactly, a drop in the great sea of life, with all personal identity lost. Not so in the teachings of Jesus. Western civilization owes its emphasis upon the importance of every individual to the Christian faith. This is where that understanding comes from. This is what nurtures that conviction. Says the Lord Christ, "There is joy in the presence of the angels of God over one sinner who repents" (Luke 15:10). Every individual is important. Even the angels celebrate when one person makes a decision for Christ!

Now look at Question Number Two: *Is God great enough to know all about us?* Is it possible He is intimately acquainted with each and every one? Or does He, in fact, exercise a kind of detached overview of what's going on, so that at best we are to Him more like ants as viewed from the twentieth story of a skyscraper?

You see, many of us find such divine knowledge staggering to imagine. It escapes our comprehension. It exceeds our grasp. After all, we have all we can do keeping track of what's going on in our own lives. Is it possible God knows what's going on in each and every life throughout this vast creation? Is the range of His knowledge that great, that incredible?

I must confess that I've wrestled with this question for years. Somehow it has bugged me. It has disturbed me—especially with my understanding of psychology and the workings of the human mind. I have found the concept of God as all-knowing to be quite challenging, to say the least. But the more I know and the more I see, the more convinced I am He can do it. He really can do it! He's got what it takes! He's got the whole world in His hands, and He's got the whole world in His mind as well! Let's see why we can say that.

For one thing, Scripture leaves no doubt about it. Again and again, the Word of God says, "He can do it! Don't you worry! He can do it!" Listen to the psalmist: "O Lord, You have searched me and known me. You know my sitting down and my rising up; You understand my thought afar off. . . . There is not a word on my tongue, But behold, O Lord, You know it altogether. . . . Such knowledge is too wonderful for me; It is high, I cannot attain it. . . . How precious also are Your thoughts to me, O God! How great is the sum of them! *If I should count them, they would be more in number than the sand.* When I awake, I am still with You" (Psalms 139:1–6, 17, 18, italics mine).

The intimate knowledge of God for each and every one of us knows no bounds! Why, God's knowledge and awareness go all the way back to the beginning, to the moment of conception! "Before I formed you in the womb I knew you," is God's Word to Jeremiah. "Before you were born I sanctified you" (Jeremiah 1:5). Jesus adds to that, saying, "Are not five sparrows sold for two copper coins? And not one of them is forgotten before God." Then He says (and since I have long since been losing hair, this impresses me), "But the very hairs of your head are all numbered" (Luke 12:6, 7). Think of that!

Throughout Scripture, the consistent testimony is that the mind which was great enough to have designed and brought into being this fantastic maze of miracles—from microcosm to macrocosm—within this vast and unaccountable universe is surely great enough to keep a close account of us. He knows us! He knows us as though He had no one else and nothing else to think about! So great is the knowledge of God! So great is His knowledge of you and me!

But now, think about this: Even apart from Scripture, we're seeing and discovering things today which make all of this fantastic stuff all the more believable. I didn't say comprehensible; I said more believable. It's still beyond comprehension. In this computer age, we're seeing things no one would have imagined a few years ago. Discovery after discovery enlarges our grasp of the limitless possibilities of life and, yes, the limitless possibilities of God.

Remember the big and bulky equipment we once used for holding knowledge? Filing cabinets. Great storage spaces. Volumes and volumes of material. All of that is obsolete now. It's a thing of the past. Why, today you can have reams of material, document upon document, stored, "remembered," on one tiny chip! Don't you find that mind-boggling? I do!

National Geographic, in an article entitled "The Electronic Mini-Marvel That Is Changing Your Life," describes the computer chip as "trifling, barely the size of a newborn's thumbnail," so light a breeze could blow it away. The backbone of it is silicon, "an ingredient," says the article, "of common beach sand. . . ." *Sand*, did you say? Wow! Remember the words of the psalmist: "How precious also are Your thoughts . . . O God! . . . If I should count them, they would be more in number than the *sand*." Tiny bits of ordinary sand can contain the marvels of the mind!

You still wonder whether the mind of God is great enough and extensive enough to know all about you and me? Wonder no more! Dismiss your doubts forever and join the ranks of the believers!

So back to the question: Does God know your name? Why, of course! What more do we need to convince us? What more do we need to take Him at His word, to take Jesus at His word? We have it on good authority through Isaiah 43:1: "Fear not, for I have redeemed you; I have called you by your name; You are Mine."

SEVEN

ANGER: DON'T LET IT THROW YOU!

WHAT DO YOU do with your anger? What is your philosophy or theory of anger control? How do you handle the powerful emotion of rage? We all experience it on occasion and in some form. We're all put to the test. How we deal with anger becomes critical. Things happen: We suffer a slight, we meet an injustice, we encounter a setback, life deals us a cruel, unmerciful blow—then anger erupts. It may come as a "slow burn" or as "spontaneous combustion." We experience tightness, a stiffening within. We get "hot under the collar," and anger takes over. It can really do us in if we let it. It can defeat our efforts and fine intentions to get it together. People have actually lost control of their lives because of unbridled anger. What then do we do? How do we deal with it?

As we look at this, notice what discerning people have said about anger. In Proverbs 16:32 we read: "He who is

61

slow to anger is better than the mighty, and he who rules his spirit than he who takes a city." Paul counseled the Ephesians in this way: "Do not let the sun go down on your wrath" (Ephesians 4:26). And the ancient Roman poet, Horace, made this stark observation: "Anger is momentary madness, so control your passion or it will control you."

Anger, you see, is potentially devastating and destructive. It is a force, a power, which literally destroys lives. Like a volcanic eruption, seething and surging from the bowels of the earth, it suddenly explodes and sends a torrent of hot, molten mass down the landscape of life, incinerating everything in its path. It can wipe us out.

But have you noticed that even though anger is destructive, it has become something of an epidemic in our time? It's so widespread that most people at one time or another seem to be angry about something or at someone. Worse than that, anger is often justified and glorified, as though to be angry were some sort of virtue. The prevalence of anger accounts for many destructive acts and activities going on throughout the world now. The violence it fosters threatens to engulf us and tear us apart: It destroys homes; it destroys society; it destroys lives. It's like a monster set loose on the contemporary scene and takes on the character of the demonic. Paul noted this character of anger when he wrote: "Do not let the sun go down on your wrath, nor give place to the devil" (Ephesians 4:26, 27).

The strange thing is that in modern times, anger has been encouraged and legitimized. It's been given the green light. It's been granted the seal of approval by the shapers of our society. There has arisen a philosophy that anger is good; it should be expressed—and the more often and the more thoroughly the better. Maybe that's the reason why it's become so widespread.

We have books telling husbands and wives how to combat each other, which, it seems to me, is but a few steps from battered wives and even battered husbands. "Let it all hang out" is the slogan. "Get it off your chest" is the motto. "Be honest" is the justification. On and on it goes, to heaven knows where.

Whatever the source of this pervasive philosophy, it is clearly at odds with good counsel from other quarters: "Do not let the sun go down on your wrath," and "He who is slow to anger is better than the mighty, and he who rules his spirit than he who takes a city." Psychiatrist John R. Marshall writes:

> There is widespread belief that if a person can be convinced, allowed, or helped to express his feelings, he will in some way benefit from it. This conviction exists at all levels of psychological sophistication. Present in one or another form, it occupies a position of central importance in almost all psychotherapies. . . . The belief that to discharge one's feelings is beneficial is also prevalent among the general public. Friends are encouraged "to get it off their chest[s]," helped to "blow off steam," or encouraged to "let it all hang out." Sports or strenuous activities are lauded as means of "working off " feelings, particularly hostility, and it is accepted that there is some value in hitting, throwing, or breaking something when one is frustrated (*Psychology Today*, November 1982).

So there you have it—the dominant, anger-condoning view of our day. That is the official sanction that nurtures and sustains the ever-increasing violence of our time as the badge of superiority rather than inferiority.

On the other hand, the destructive power of anger is well attested to and documented. A proneness to anger contributes to poor health and leads to early death. It is a highly effective means of self-destruction. Dr. Carrol A. Wise has said: "Anger, if intense and if allowed to become chronic, does burn us out, making love impossible and leaving a marked sense of insecurity and emptiness. It leads to illness in one form or another. Human relationships grounded in these feelings destroy; it is as if man expects to nourish his body on poison."

Recently there has come to my attention the findings of research at Duke University as reported by Dr. Redfield Williams, Jr., at a seminar sponsored by the American Heart Association. The findings were these: People who live with anger and are prone to anger are *five times* more likely to have heart disease. A basic distrust of other people, a tendency to find fault and to yield to minor irritants, and a frequent display of anger contribute to artery disease and the likelihood of earlier death. Anger is destructive. Anger kills people!

Not only is anger destructive, new research strongly suggests that its expression as a kind of catharsis may not be the best approach. This is not to say we should not at times get things out in the open. Nor is it to say there is no benefit in verbalizing our feelings, objectifying them. Nor again is it to say some of us may not need to spend time with a counselor where we do, in fact, get things off our chest, particularly when the anger is very deep. But as a style of life, as a way of characteristically conducting ourselves, it is ineffective and counterproductive.

What is now discovered is this: To express anger is to

practice anger and to get "better" at it. To practice anger is to become a chronically unhappy person. "Getting it off your chest" may not, in fact, get it off your chest; it may instead make the weight heavier on your chest. It may reinforce it, intensify it, and make you a rather unpleasant person to have around. Who wants negative people in his presence? Hostility invites hostility. Anger invites anger. It does you more harm than good. Here's a handy way to think about its actual effect:

> When you express it, you impress it.
> When you release it, you increase it.
> When you vent it, you repent it.

In other words, it's not the way to live! Nor is it the way to deal with anger effectively. "The psychological rationale for ventilating anger does not stand up under experimental scrutiny," states a report in *Psychology Today* (November 1982). "The weight of evidence indicates precisely the opposite: Expressing anger makes you angrier, solidifies an angry attitude, and establishes a hostile habit."

What's the answer then? The answer is with Paul and Solomon and Jesus Christ: "Do not let the sun go down on your wrath." "He who is slow to anger is better than the mighty, and he who rules his spirit than he who takes a city." "Whoever is angry with his brother. . . ," states our Lord, "shall be in danger of the judgment" (Matthew 5:22). The answer is the cultivation of a spirit of faith, good will, serenity, and love.

Surely we need to acknowledge and discover the seeds of anger before the bitter harvest. We need to be alert to why we're angry and what there is about ourselves that makes us susceptible to anger. But most of all, we need to cultivate a spirit of inner strength and outer poise that comes through a sense of the power and presence of Christ.

What, then, do we do with anger? First, *we must decide to deal with it.* We emphatically make that decision. We won't ignore the anger. We won't deny it. We won't pretend it isn't there. We won't cover it up or repress it. Rather, we acknowledge its presence and resolve to come to terms with it.

A woman wrote me the other day saying she needed help dealing with her anger. I did not know her. She did not belong to my church; nor did she live in my community. She had written because she had read something I had written. She related that her husband had had an affair. Almost as soon as he had gotten into it, he realized it was wrong and tried to make amends. She was grateful that he had come to his senses. He returned to her and acknowledged the wrong and deeply regretted the incident. But now, she told me, she has to deal with her anger, particularly against the woman who had led her husband on into this infidelity that had violated their marriage.

That troubled woman was moving in the right direction—dealing directly with her anger by recognizing the problem and realizing that she had to do something about it. Failure to deal with it would eventually poison and probably destroy her marriage. That's exactly why she wrote me: because she wanted to do something to change her situation.

Second, *we must get at the root cause.* In the case of this woman, it was immediately clear what the cause was. But other times it's not so clear. It takes a little exploration. "Why am I reacting this way?" we ask ourselves. "What's bugging me? What's disturbing me? What's my problem?" Sometimes the simple identification of the cause puts anger to flight. Other times it doesn't. Then we need to do more, but at least we know where to focus our attention, what we have to work on.

Third, insofar as possible, *we must uproot the cause.* We remove it. We get rid of it. We change what needs changing. We correct what needs correcting. We make our peace with whatever is creating unrest. We take definite and constructive action to make needed changes. We take steps to put things right.

Jesus gives an example of this in the Sermon on the Mount. "Therefore," prescribes the Great Physician, "if you bring your gift to the altar, and there remember that your brother has something against you, leave your gift there before the altar, and go your way. First be reconciled to your brother, and then come and offer your gift" (Matthew 5:23, 24).

Good advice! It's sound! It means *take action.* Insofar as is possible, eradicate the cause of your anger.

Fourth, *we must see more deeply into life.* We see ourselves for what we are. We note our utterly human tendencies—the hurts and needs, the fears and anguish— which make us anger-prone, which upset us. We try to understand the other person—whoever it may be that perhaps is connected with our anger or may even be the supposed "cause" of it. We try to understand, as sympathetically as possible, what's going on within him or her. Seeing the other person with empathetic eyes can change everything. Often these lines cross my mind when I am trying to help people deal with their feelings:

> If I knew you and you knew me—
> If both of us could clearly see,
> And with an inner sight divine
> The meaning of your heart and mine—
> I'm sure that we should differ less
> And clasp our hands in friendliness—
> Our thoughts would pleasantly agree,
> If I knew you and you knew me.
>
> NIXON WATERMAN

Fifth, *we must commit the anger to God.* Let it go! Let it get lost in the vast sea of divine grace and forgiveness. Let our daily ritual be this: through the day, but certainly and unfailingly at the end of the day, to rid our hearts of lingering animosity and ill will. Turn it all over to Him and be done with it!

Dr. Paul Tournier, the Swiss psychiatrist who has seen so well the connection between Christian faith and personal well-being, has related this story of a young woman in his book *The Healing of Persons*: "I was nervous and high-strung," she said, "going rapidly from a period of enthusiasm to one of depression, always having ups and downs—tiring both to myself and to those I was with. . . . I had very little self-control, and used to give way to all my feelings—anger, enthusiasm, or despair—not without a certain violence, in a way which was painful to people about me. [Then] I began to pray, to obey; and my life began to be centered on Jesus Christ. . . .

"There came a day," she continued, "when I realized that a new balance had been established in my body—an evenness of temper. . . . This new state of mind depends on my regular quiet times and my surrender to God. It isn't something acquired once and for all, but it remains and lasts in the measure to which I obey God, confess him, and am freed from my sins. The health of my body depends upon the health of my soul." This is how we turn it over to God, and we seek His forgiveness.

Let me conclude this chapter with a deeply moving story. A friend in the ministry lost his son a few years ago. The boy was away at college at the time, and he and some friends had gone to a public place near the college. As they were leaving and heading for the car, my friend's son realized he had left his keys in the building. He and one of his friends started back. As they did so, they passed a group of thugs. Just then, one of the bullies called out to another: "Here's your chance! Let's see what you can do!" With that, one of them jumped my friend's son, intending to beat him up. A scuffle took place. His friend and another, rushing over from the car, joined in. In short order, they had the thugs pinned to the ground. Thinking that was the end of it, they got up and let their assailants loose. Suddenly one of the thugs pulled out a gun and shot all three, killing my friend's son on the spot.

At the time of this tragic incident, my minister friend was attending the Robert Schuller Institute at the Crystal Cathedral in Garden Grove, California. When the word came, those at the institute surrounded my friend with love and compassion. They did everything they could for him. They helped him in every conceivable way. He was profoundly moved by their caring.

When he returned home, he received a long-distance call from Robert Schuller, who talked with him for a half hour. As my friend related this episode to me, I asked him, "What did Dr. Schuller say to you?" My friend answered, "He said, 'I want you to know we have been thinking of you and praying for you.' He asked me how it happened, and when I finished telling him, he said, 'What can I do to help you?' I answered, 'I don't know of anything, except possibly how to deal with the anger I feel.' Then Dr. Schuller said to me, 'Julius, when you feel anger coming over you, stop a moment and pray to God, thanking Him for the privilege of having your son for twenty-one wonderful years!' "

Turn it over to God! That's the best thing you can do! In a spirit of thankfulness for whatever good has come your way, relinquish your anger to His divine mercy and grace. Don't let it get in the way of living. Don't let it throw you, jeopardize all your wonderful efforts to get your life together. Let it go—*forever!*

EIGHT

IT'S TRUST OR BUST

HOW TRUSTING ARE you? Is it important to trust? Is it a weakness or a strength to be trusting? Are trusting people more gullible, or might they, in fact, be less gullible? How would you answer? Where would you come out? These are crucial questions. They all have to do with living a happy, fulfilling, productive life. They are critical as you get your life together.

We had an example of trust at a service in our church not long ago. It happened during an infant baptism which I was conducting. Now, of course, babies react differently to the experience. Some are perfectly happy; others make a noisy protest. Some are as sweet as can be; others are cantankerous. But on this Sunday, we had a young man of seven months who acted like a pro. It didn't bother him one bit. He was happy. He was relaxed. He was all smiles. Why? Simple! He had trust. Why did he have trust? Probably because he recognized it was his grandfather who

71

was baptizing him! We got along beautifully. Ours was a relationship of trust.

Yet here are striking words from the psalmist on the subject of trust: "It is better to trust in the Lord than to put confidence in man. It is better to trust in the Lord than to put confidence in princes" (Psalms 118:8, 9). What did the writer mean? What was he getting at?

There's no question about it: Trust can be beneficial. An experience of trust can turn a life around. A respected English clergyman told the story of his life to J. Wallace Hamilton. This is the way he put it:

> The turning point in my life came when I was seventeen years old. I was called the black sheep in the family. We were always fighting each other. One night they were all picking on me: my mother, my father, my brother, and my sister, until I could stand it no more. I jumped up and cried: "I'm leaving; I'm getting out of here." I ran up the stairs and there suddenly in the darkened hallway, I ran into my grandmother. She had listened to it all. The diatribes, the accusations, the vilifications. She stood in the hallway and stopped me by putting her hand on my shoulder. With tears in her eyes she said the words that changed my life. "John, I believe in you."

To believe in someone is to trust that person. To trust someone can change that person's life!

On the other hand, the absence of trust can be devastating. It can destroy a life. You wonder about that? Think about this: An elderly woman was living alone in her second-floor apartment. She had become a withdrawn, fearful recluse. She cut herself off from everyone. She lived so much to herself that when she died nobody knew about it. When neighbors began to wonder why they hadn't seen her, they called the police who entered the apartment and found the poor woman's badly decomposed body. They found more: They found stacks and stacks of rubbish and garbage that reached the ceiling. Amid it all, the desperate woman had made little aisles by which she could make her way through the cluttered rooms in her final days. What happened? Why did this woman live and die so tragically? For one simple reason: She didn't trust anybody! She had become so distrusting and paranoid, she severed all human contacts and died alone in the midst of waste! The absence of trust can be ruinous to a life.

Of course, sometimes people take advantage of our trust. I suppose that was how one teenager felt while talking with a friend about a breakup with her boyfriend. "Not only has he broken my heart and destroyed my life," she cried, "he ruined my whole evening."

I suppose you could call it a betrayal of trust that was expressed in a conversation between two cannibal chiefs after a delicious dinner: "Your wife sure makes a wonderful pot roast," said the one. "Yes," responded the other, "but I'm sure going to miss her!"

At any rate, here's the first thing we need to get straight: **Trust is essential to healthy, happy, productive living.** This is absolutely true. To be the best you can be, you need to be trusting. Here's why: Psychologists have studied the role of trust in human life. They've made a fascinating discovery. They posed questions like, "Are trusting people more, or less, gullible?" Then they did their studies. They learned that nontrusting people are *more likely* to be taken in or deceived! Why is that? Because of their rigid outlook, born of suspicion, which makes them less perceptive, less aware, less discriminating. They are blinded by their own misperception of reality due to a lack of trust. Moreover, they miss many of life's greatest opportunities. Dr. Paul Tournier, the noted Swiss psychiatrist, once said to a patient: "I cannot help you unless there is established between you and me a feeling of complete trust." So trust is necessary for healthy, happy, and productive living.

Here is the second thing we need to understand: *We can nonetheless be deceived.* That's the risk we take. That's life! Sure, people will sometimes let us down. People will sometimes disappoint us. But we accept that and make the best of it. One thing we don't do: We don't turn sour and become jaundiced about life! We realize it's more important to maintain an attitude of trust than to become cynical and withdrawn like the tragic woman who died alone in her filth-filled apartment.

Several weeks ago, I had occasion to write a check for a new automobile battery. I was out-of-town at the time, and the manager of the service station where I stopped did not know me. When she realized I was a minister (which I conveniently brought to her attention in hopes she would accept my check!), she decided to give me the benefit of the doubt. Then she showed me an unpaid bill in her cash register. It was that of a minister, no less, who had assured her he would come back and pay it. Sadly, that had been many months before, and the fellow had not appeared yet. Did I know this man, she asked. I acknowledged I did not, but I did point out, for her benefit, that you can't even always trust ministers! Let that be a lesson to you!

People will let us down. We know that. We accept that. As people of faith, we know something about the goodness of life and people, but we also know something about the human tendency toward sin and corruption. We are realists, but we're certainly not going to get cynical about it!

So where does that bring us? Back to this, I suppose: "It is better to trust in the Lord than to put confidence in man. It is better to trust in the Lord than to put confidence in princes."

Here is the third thing we need to get clear: *the extreme importance of provisional trust.* Having seen, on the one hand, that trust is essential to living and what comes of a lack of it, and having seen, on the other hand, that there are risks, there are dangers, now we need to see that to operate productively in life, we must go ahead and take our chances anyway.

This means that as people of faith, if we are to err, we're going to err on the side of trust. It's a positive choice. It's a positive approach. It provides the optimum chance of things coming out right most of the time.

Twenty-five years ago, I was trying to help a man who was an alcoholic. We were working on his problem together on a daily basis. Day after day, I visited with him and we prayed together. We would review his situation and how he was progressing. We would look ahead to one more day of success. He was making headway. We were both elated as the days and weeks of abstinence piled up. Then came a critical decision.

I got a call from his wife who had been most supportive of our efforts. She was being called away to be with their daughter who was soon to have a baby, her first child. She needed her mother. This meant the wife of this man would travel a great distance and be totally out of the picture for some time. He would be alone for several weeks. Should she risk it? Should she take the chance of leaving her husband by himself for that extended period of time?

Would he be tempted, once alone in the house, to take a drink and thus ruin everything we had accomplished together?

Believe me, this was a tough decision. A lot was at stake. Weeks and weeks of hard work might go down the drain. But after a moment's reflection and prayer, I said: "Yes! Now's the time for the test. Now's the time to take a chance, to show him we trust him. If he makes it, he'll be stronger and surer than ever before! I think he can handle it!" So she left, went to be with her daughter, and, yes, he came through! He came through marvelously, in fact. To the end of his life (he died a year ago, nearly twenty-five years later), he never again took a drink!

You see, we have to operate with provisional trust— with others, with our children, with one another, with life—in order to make headway. We have to take a chance. We have to be willing to take risks. It's the only way!

But there's a fourth thing we need to understand fully: *the absolute importance of an ultimate trust!* You see, we have to base our trust on something. We have to build it on something. It can't rest on air. It can't sit on quicksand. It's got to have a solid foundation if it is to be secure. Somewhere in the midst of life we must find the foundational basis for our trust, for being trusting toward others, for being trusting toward life, for keeping the lines open and our lives growing and expansive.

Where is that basis to be found? In human nature? No. We know better than that. In ourselves? Are you kidding? We're only human. We let ourselves down sometimes. Boy, do we let ourselves down! No, we need something more ultimate than any of these. We need God! We need Christ! There, and there alone, is our ultimate security, our ultimate assurance, our ultimate trust!

Isn't that what the psalmist was trying to say? Isn't that where we must come out? "It is better to trust in the Lord than to put confidence in man. It is better to trust in the Lord than to put confidence in princes."

There's another great passage that says the same thing. It's Proverbs 3:5, 6: "Trust in the Lord with all your heart, and lean not on your own understanding; in all your ways acknowledge Him, and He shall direct your paths."

Believe me, friend, it's the only way. Believe me, it's **trust or bust!** Believe me, God alone is the sound basis of our hope and trust, for He alone will see us through to the end! I believe that. Do you?

Henry Ward Beecher recalled a very difficult time in his life as a boy. His family was struggling to make ends meet. His mother was typically fearful and doubting, but his father, Lyman, refused to surrender to despair. Mrs. Beecher predicted they would end up in the poor house. Lyman responded: "My dear, I have trusted God now for forty years, and He has never forsaken me, and I am not going to begin to distrust Him now." Young Henry, hearing that statement, never forgot it. As long as he lived, that single sentence stood out in his memory.

Where is your ultimate security? Where do you *place* your trust? Where do you *base* your trust? Let faith call you to complete surrender to Jesus Christ! He will never let you down!

NINE

WHEN YOU'RE TEMPTED TO QUIT

ONE OF LIFE'S foremost temptations is the temptation to quit. It's the temptation to give up and give in. It's a common enough urge. Maybe things haven't gone as we had hoped. Maybe we're not making the progress we'd counted on. Maybe we've met setbacks and disappointments. Maybe our fondest dream has been dashed. Then we've said, "What's the use? Where's it getting me? I give up! I throw in the towel! I quit!"

We see this in the man who has worked many years toward certain objectives, toward the fulfillment of ambitions and hopes. But things have turned against him. He sees ahead the possibility of defeat, the effort of many years going down the drain. He's tempted to quit. Or in the youth trying to make headway in school, striving for academic excellence. Yet, for all those efforts, the results have not paid off. He or she is tempted to quit. Or in the woman devoting herself to worthy undertakings of social service. But recently she's met with resistance, failure, lack of cooperation. She's begun to feel it's hopeless. She's tempted to quit. Or once more, we see it in the fine person trying to live for what is right, decent, and honest. Yet there have been reversals. People in general seem indifferent to the values that seem important to him. This person is discouraged by widespread apathy, entrenched corruption, powerful opposition. That person is tempted to quit.

Longfellow, in his poem "Soliloquy on the Bridge," has caught the mood:

> How often, O how often,
> In the days that had gone by,
> I had stood on the bridge at midnight,
> And looked on the wave and sky;
> How often, O how often,
> I had wished that the ebbing tide
> Would bear me away on its bosom
> To the ocean wild and wide;
> For my heart was hot and restless
> And my mind was full of care,
> And the burden that laid upon me
> Seemed greater than I could bear.

Does that describe how you have felt? Does it describe how you are feeling now? Can you identify with that mood? You've been trying, really trying, but you haven't tasted the sweet joy of success. You've been plugging away, but, to date, the breakthrough hasn't come. You're beginning to wonder whether it's worth it, whether it's worth all the effort. Just now, you're ready to give up, ready to quit, ready to settle back and drift away. If that's your story, watch out! This is a dangerous time. It's the one time you must not quit!

I was talking one day with a dear and close friend of many years. Not long before our conversation, he had reached the zenith of his career and was enjoying national recognition. Just then, he had been stricken with a serious circulatory condition. This required the immediate amputation of a leg, followed by a long ordeal of getting accustomed to an artificial limb. Through it all, he suffered intense pain, and thereafter, though he had learned to move about with amazing skill, he experienced discomfort and pain much of the time. As we talked, he confided that some people had said, "How we admire your courage!" "Courage?" he admitted to me he was inclined to reply. "Is it courage? Or is it a will to survive? What happens to you," he added, "if you give up? What becomes of you if you quit?"

A temptation? Yes! And a most serious one at that! It's a temptation which if yielded to, can ruin all our efforts. It can scuttle all our dreams and plans. It can put life on the skids and leave us on the side of the road, stranded, getting nowhere. So what do you do when you find yourself at that critical point, on the edge of despondency and resignation? What do you do when you're tempted to quit?

First, *check your fatigue factor.* Maybe you're just tired, worn out. Maybe you need rest. Frequently when we get discouraged, when we feel ill-equipped to face life, the root of the problem is simple fatigue. We've allowed ourselves to get exhausted—physically, emotionally, or both. We've neglected our rest. We haven't taken time out. We haven't had a change of scenery. Physically and emotionally spent, we decline in output and outlook.

When that's the case, one thing is certain. This is not the time for important changes or great decisions, not even the decision to quit. Any decision is likely to be a bad one, negatively influenced by our subjective state. We're in no frame of mind to make good judgments. What we need now is rest, relaxation, and renewal. Dr. Paul Dudley White, the noted heart specialist who combined good sense with expertise, once said: "We don't need to make a fetish of health habits, but we must recognize that our somatic deficiencies can not only shorten our lives but depress our spirits." So, when you're tempted to quit, start by checking the fatigue factor.

Second, *review your objectives.* What, after all, do you want? What are your hopes and goals and purposes? What are you seeking? Are those goals still valid? Are they still worth seeking? Do you really want to give up on them just now? Maybe you've forgotten them? Maybe you've lost sight of your objectives. Maybe you've allowed them to recede into the shadows, though they remain just as sound and legitimate and inviting. So why not recollect them, reinstate them, polish them up, reaffirm them?

As a young man I studied voice to become a better singer. One challenge in singing is getting through a long phrase on a single breath. Sometimes you can't do it; you have to take a "catch breath," but it's better not to. Good singers sustain the voice all the way on a single breath. One day during a voice lesson, I was having difficulty with such a phrase. Somehow I couldn't make it to the end. When I asked my teacher how to handle the situation, she made a neat suggestion. "Think to the end," she said. "Think to the end of the phrase." Sure enough, it worked! From then on, whenever I confronted such a challenge, I would "think to the end." But now, isn't that simply focusing on your objective? It's another way of saying, "Remember your objectives."

Twenty years ago, a national magazine carried an article devoted to the complaints of a former teacher who had left the teaching profession. A couple of weeks later, the

"Letters to the Editor" column carried a reply. It was sent in by another teacher who gave this indictment of her fellow professionals: "Why is it," she asked, "that the quitters get the attention of the publishers and the sympathy of people. I, too, am a teacher. I began to teach at a junior high school in Manhattan. All the lady complains about are there—poor facilities, pressure of administrative duties, unruly, disturbed, not too bright children; and I cannot refute her argument. The teacher's college doesn't prepare one for keeping order among thirty-seven growing adolescents. But a good teacher goes on the principle that the need is our call. Are we teachers to wait for ideal conditions to live in an un-ideal world?"

When you're tempted to quit, "think to the end," review your objectives.

Third, *recover the power of your original inspiration.* Somewhere back there, you had moments of clarity, moments of vision, moments of inspiration. They were probably times when your perception was clearest, when your outlook was sharpest, and when you felt the sustaining, surging power that could see you through. Paul often told how his moment of greatest inspiration was on the road to Damascus. It was then that the Lord Christ spoke to him and he became a changed man. That single experience drove and sustained him the rest of his life. Recall how, just before he was taken to Rome as a prisoner many years later, he stood before King Agrippa, the Roman tetrarch, and told of that experience and what it meant to his life. Recall how he summed it up: "Therefore, King Agrippa, I was not disobedient to the heavenly vision" (Acts 26:19). Paul kept the power of that vision alive to the end!

At another time, the great Apostle made the suggestion to young Timothy: "Stir up the gift of God which is in you . . ." (2 Timothy 1:6). Stir up that earlier inspiration. Keep alive that earlier vision. Great advice! It reminds me of the new boarder in a boarding house. When he came to the dinner table and joined his fellow boarders for the first time, he was closely watched by the landlady. When he began to put sugar in his coffee, she kept an eagle eye on him. He took one cube, then a second, then a third, then a fourth, and even a fifth. Finally, this was too much for the landlady who called out, "Why don't you stir it up?" "Who wants it sweet?" he shot back. To get back your motivation, stir up the vision. Recover the power of your original inspiration.

Fourth, *keep up your persistence.* Don't lose the benefit of old-fashioned perseverance. It is a personal quality that serves us well. Simple persistence can win the day when all else fails. Hang on by your teeth! A former parishioner in one of my Vermont churches sent me a quotation from that well-known and oft-quoted Vermonter, "Cal" Coolidge. It fits our point here. "Nothing in the world can take the place of persistence. Talent will not: nothing is more common than unsuccessful men with talent. Genius will not: unrewarded genius is almost a proverb. Education will not: the world is full of educated derelicts. Persistence and determination alone are omnipotent. The slogan 'Press on' has solved and always will solve the problems of the human race." That from the presidential sage of Plymouth, Vermont.

Years ago I came upon this brief verse which, to me, catches the spirit beautifully:

If all my ships go out to sea
And never come back to me,
If I must watch from day to day
An empty waste of waters grey—
Then I shall fashion one ship more
From bits of driftwood on the shore,
I'll build that ship with toil and pain
And send it out to sea again!

So here's the message: When you're tempted to quit, don't lose the benefit of old-fashioned, dogged perseverance. Keep up your persistence!

And finally, by all means, *sense the enveloping presence of God.* Bask in His Spirit. Become open to His inflooding power. Realize again and again that around you and in you and through you is the Divine Force which can hold and sustain you to the end. When young Peter Marshall—one of the most gifted and dedicated preachers America has ever known, and for many years chaplain of the United States Senate—first came to America, he had struggles. He had difficult times. He shared their impact in letters he wrote home to his mother in Scotland. He noted that people had spoken of his apparent courage since he was alone in a strange land, among strange people, and far from family and friends in his native Scotland. "They little know," said he to his mother, "that I am never alone, for I feel that my every action is guided by Him who ordains all things for His servants, and supplies all their needs."

Absolutely! This above all we can count on, that holding us up and keeping us from quitting is the strong and abiding sense of the enveloping presence of God. Believe that! Never allow your consciousness of it to abate!

If you stand very still in the depths of a wood
You will hear many wonderful things:
The snap of a twig, the wind in the trees,
The whir of invisible wings.

If you stand very still at a difficult hour
And wait for the silence within,
You then will be led in wisdom and strength
Through a world of confusion and din.

If year after year you keep inwardly still,
God will bring you the help that you ask,
In the silence He gives you will find what you need—
His wisdom, His strength, for each task.

TEN

IS WORRY YOUR PROBLEM?

LET ME BEGIN this chapter with an embarrassing confession. My good and treasured friend Bruce Larson was guest speaker at our services in Wethersfield one Sunday morning a couple of years ago. For the first half of the service, he was seated at the lower level, but for the sermon he would climb stairs to the high pulpit of our Colonial New England Meetinghouse. Now, there's a pulpit "ten feet above contradiction"! There are seven steps up the stairway, and at the top there is a door to be opened and to be shut as you enter the pulpit and prepare to preach. I had alerted Bruce to this "obstacle course to heaven," and anticipated he would go up early during the hymn beforehand, allowing plenty of time to move into the sermon.

Now, Bruce Larson is an extraordinarily relaxed human being. I love him for it. He has taught me so much about life in grace, I can never say enough for what he has contributed to my life. More than anyone I know, he has understood what Paul was talking about when the Apostle of Freedom spoke of the life of liberty in the Spirit. But from time to time, I need to be reminded, and Bruce Larson, more than anyone, reminds me by his own contagious style. He keeps me aware of the fantastic freedom and joy we have in the life of faith.

During the first service, Bruce took his time heading up the stairway. In fact, the hymn was nearly over before he started. He made it, of course, and his message was terrific. He was his usual magnificent, engaging self. Nonetheless, I was watchful and a little uneasy about his getting up the pulpit stairs.

So during the second service, as the ushers were receiving the offering, I leaned over to Bruce and suggested he plan to start up a little sooner. He looked at me, with a direct and penetrating expression, and said, "Why?"

What could I say? That I was afraid he wouldn't make it? "Because I worry," I said, hoping to get through a delicate moment.

To that, he said, "*You* have a problem!"

Bless his heart, he was right! Boy, was he right! Why should I worry about his getting up the stairs and into the morning message unscathed? Right away, I knew I had been unfaithful!

Bruce said I had a problem, and at the time he was right. What about you? Is worry your problem? Is worrying getting in the way of your living joyfully, creatively, serenely? It will do it, of course. It will consume energy, reduce effectiveness, curtail your capacity for doing great things. It's one more thing we need to look at if we're going to get it together and take off!

Did you know Jesus was against worry? He tried to banish it among His believers. He says, "Don't worry!" (Matthew 6:25 TLB.) That is, kick the worry habit! "Don't worry about *things*—food, drink, and clothes." Or, for that matter, all the other pointless things people worry about. "Don't worry!" Then He says, "For you already have life and a body—and they are far more important than what to eat and wear." ***"Don't worry!"*** Then He makes this arresting observation: "Will all your worries add a single moment to your life?" The answer, obviously, is *no!* In fact, the opposite is the case: Worries shorten life, worries disable life, worries make us miserable! So, "don't worry!" That's what Jesus says.

Have you ever seen worry beads? I was given some years ago by a friend who had been to India. Apparently they're plentiful over there. They're quite handy. You can handle them without thinking. They keep your hands busy but they accomplish nothing. They simply use up energy, as you worry about things. That's all worry beads are good for—using up energy. That's all *worry* is good for—using up energy. But think of this: We could use that energy in better ways. So, "don't worry," said the Master of Life.

Listen to how 1 Peter 5:7 puts it: "Let Him have all your worries and cares" (TLB). The Amplified Version puts it more forcefully: "Casting the whole of your care—all your anxieties, all your concerns, once and for all—on Him; for He cares for you affectionately, and cares about you watchfully."

Yet, with all those wonderful assurances, we're inclined to answer back: "Why **not** worry? Think of all the things we have to worry about!" Some wag said, "If you're not worrying, you don't know the situation!" "Things are bad!" we may insist. "Things are uncertain. How can we not worry?"

The issue is not whether there are things to worry about. There are! Plenty of things, in the world and in our personal lives. The central issue is: What *good* will worry do? The central issue is: What does worry accomplish? "Will all your worries add a single moment to your life?" asks Jesus. We know the answer.

Then the issue is: What *harm* does it do? If it doesn't do any good, does it do any harm? That puts it in quite a different light. "Worry," said William A. Ward, "distorts our thinking, disrupts our work, disquiets our soul, disturbs our body, disfigures our face, destroys our poise, depresses our friends, demoralizes our life, defeats our faith, and debilitates our energy." If worry doesn't do us any good, it sure does us a lot of harm!

Someone with a humorous touch designed what he calls a "Worry Table." It's a useful way to categorize worries so we can manage them better. He notes that they fall into five classifications:

First, worries about disasters which, as later events prove, never happened. About 40 percent of our worries.

Second, worries about decisions I had made in the past, decisions about which I could now of course do nothing. About 30 percent of my worries.

Third, worries about possible sickness and a possible nervous breakdown, neither of which materialized. About 12 percent of my worries.

Fourth, worries about my children and my friends, worries arising from the fact I forgot these people have an ordinary amount of common sense. About 10 percent of my worries.

Fifth, worries that have a real foundation. Possibly 8 percent of the total.

You see how it comes out. We could nicely reduce worrying to nothing more than the fifth category, thus eliminating in one fell swoop 92 percent of our worries! That would be a dramatic improvement! It's always good to reduce things to bite size, then you have a small deal rather than a big one.

"I'm supposed to tell you," said a boy to his father, "that there's a small Parent/Teacher's meeting tomorrow night at school."

"Well, if it's going to be small," replied the father, "do I need to go?"

"I guess so," answered the boy. "It's just between you, me, the teacher, and the principal." That sounds like a manageable meeting!

The "Sage of Concord," Ralph Waldo Emerson, put worry in this helpful context:

> Some of your hurts you have cured,
>   And the sharpest you still have survived,
> But what torments of grief you endured
>   From evils that never arrived!

Now, let me make a suggestion. If your problem is worry, try submitting your worries to five critical tests: the test of time, the test of geography, the test of importance, the test of priorities, and the test of faith.

First, **the test of time.** If the thing you're worrying about does happen, what will it matter in the long run? What difference will it make later on? In a year? In ten years? That's a bit of wisdom my older brother, the one who spoke those all-important words when our mother had died, passed on to me years ago when I was a teenager. It has served me well. You'd be surprised how many worries get nipped in the bud if we simply say, "How will I feel about it a year from now? Will I even remember it?" An unknown author expressed the technique like this:

Take yesterday's worries and sort them all out,
And you'll wonder whatever you worried about.
Look back at the cares that once furrowed your brow,
I fancy you'll smile at most of them now.
They seemed so terrible then, but they really were not,
For once out of the woods, all the fears are forgot.

Second, subject those worries to *the test of geography.* Are they really your concern? Are they really on your turf? Or are they quite beyond your control, outside your domain? In other words, beware of borrowing trouble. Many of us are anxious because of overexposure to the world's ills. Through the invention of television, we are subjected to every calamity under the sun. Someone said, "The road to hell is paved by good *inventions.*" Well, TV does get a little hellish at times! How much can we take? How much should we absorb? Certainly the situation calls for selectivity. It calls for discrimination. Even our TV set is constantly screening out signals it does not want to accept for the sake of one clear, sometimes beautiful, intelligible signal. Can we do less? To be sure, there are larger concerns for us to address, to become acquainted with, and to seek to answer in association with others. That's constructive! But God doesn't expect us to be the saviors of the world. He's already taken care of that Himself! No, focus on concerns which are rightly yours, on your own turf, in your own domain, subject to your control. Put those worries to the test of geography.

Third, subject those worries to *the test of importance.* Are they worth the bother? Or are they trivial? What petty things we let ourselves worry about! And for what purpose? Jesus counseled against preoccupation with trivia in

His remarks in the Sermon on the Mount. Look at the big picture, He was saying. Look at what's really important. It's the old adage, don't make mountains out of molehills.

> Worry—is like a distant hill
>   We glimpse against the sky.
> We wonder how we ever will
>   Get up a hill so high.
>
> Yet, when we reach the top, we see
>   The roadway left behind
> Is not as steep or sheer as we
>   Have pictured in our mind.
>
> AUTHOR UNKNOWN

Fourth, subject those worries to **the test of your priorities.** What are you living for? What are your goals, your objectives, your dreams? How can you best serve those? Not by scattering your attention over the landscape. Not by diffusing your energies in too many directions. And what is God's plan for you and your life? Get your priorities clearly in mind and resolutely refuse to worry about things which have no bearing upon them! "I am always happy," said a woman in the north country of England, "and my secret is always to sail the seas, and ever to keep my heart in port."

And last, subject your worries to **the test of faith.** Jesus identified worry as faithlessness. It's a sign of a lack of faith. E. Stanley Jones said, "Worry or fear is a kind of atheism." Further, he has said that "the Christian has expunged worry from his vocabulary." Now, that brings the whole matter down to the final test. What is faith? Isn't it trust? Isn't it total and trusting reliance upon God?

There is a phrase that captures the heart of it: "In all things resigned to His will." So our job is simple: We let it happen. We go with the flow. We relax and let the Spirit coursing through our lives and through events show us the way. "In all things, resigned to His will."

So, *why worry?*

You see what this means? Our job is like that of the actor upon the stage who said his task was simple: just remember his lines and not trip over the furniture. All we have to do is equally simple: just get ourselves and our egos out of the way and let God run the show. Lots of things begin to happen then. Lots of things go better when we get that central concept of faith operational! "In all things, resigned to His will."

So, *why worry?*

> Trust in the Lord with all your heart,
> And lean not on your own understanding;
> In all your ways acknowledge Him,
> And He shall direct your paths.
>
> Proverbs 3:5, 6

So, *why worry?*

"Why should I worry?" asked Simone Weil. "It's not my business to think of myself. My business is to think of God. It's His business to think of me."

So, *why worry?*

Said Donald Hankey to his men as he led them against the enemy during World War I: "If you're hit, it's Blighty. If you're killed, it's the Resurrection."

So, *why worry?*

I read somewhere of a young boy who during a trans-Atlantic voyage seemed astonishingly undisturbed during a fierce storm that clearly troubled the other passengers on the ocean liner. "Son, aren't you afraid?" inquired a mystified man. "No, sir," said the boy, smiling and confident. "You see, my father is the captain."

So, *why worry?*

The words of the Bach chorale give the message of serenity and final assurance:

> Therefore I thank my God, and joy to do His will;
> I know, whate'er befalls, His love doth lead me still.
> So like a little child, who clasps his father's hand,
> Serene I take my way; in faith untroubled stand.

ELEVEN

YOU CAN LICK DEPRESSION!

ARE YOU SAD? That's spelled S–A–D in capital letters. I don't mean simply unhappy. I mean what I've said— SAD. Are you manifesting what is called the Seasonal Affective Syndrome—or seasonal depression? Are you depressed? Have you experienced depression lately? Have some of the things you've been through caused you to feel depressed? If so, I have news for you: You can lick it!

Of course, the acronym SAD refers to seasons of the year when we're susceptible to depression, like January or mid-winter. That's when people sometimes have "the January blahs." Whatever the tag, many suffer this condition—some seasonally, some recurringly, some chronically. It's the foremost emotional problem people face. But whatever it is, it can be licked! It can be defeated! It can be overcome!

Who has not asked the question of the psalmist: "Why are you cast down, O my soul? And why are you disquieted within me?" (Psalms 42:5.) All of us, at one time or another, feel down. We may even feel depressed. But we can lick it!

But first, what's depression? What is this "dark night of the soul," as Saint John of the Cross put it? Certainly it is deep discouragement, a persistent feeling of "what's the use?" It is deepening despair, hopelessness and helplessness, maybe a loss of all emotional feeling. We may feel exhausted, worn out. We don't see how we can go on. That's depression. There are two major causes, according to Dr. Willard Gaylin. One is a loss of confidence *in* ourselves; the other is a loss of respect *for* ourselves. We feel worthless and we feel powerless. So we subject ourselves to inner abuse. We say, "I'm no good. I can't do anything right. I'll never get anywhere." Powerless! Worthless! So depressed! But remember—it can be licked!

Now, let me say this: If you're feeling really bad, if your depression seems too heavy or frightening or persistent, then seek help! You wouldn't refuse help if you were drowning. You wouldn't refuse help if your house were on fire. You wouldn't refuse help if you had acute appendicitis. You wouldn't refuse help if you were at the bottom of a well and your life was about to be snuffed out. Why refuse help if you are tormented by persistent, deepening, unyielding depression?

It's not a sign of weakness to ask for help. To the contrary, it's a sign of strength. It's not a sign of stupidity to consult another person—a minister, a doctor, a psychologist, a psychiatrist. It's a sign of wisdom. It's sheer problem-solving. You have a problem. You want to solve it. It's not a denial of God to seek help, as though you and He alone should work it out. Rather, it's an affirmation of faith that God works everywhere. God is everywhere. "God moves in a mysterious way, His wonders to perform," through many things and many people. In fact, when and if the thought "I need help" comes to you, it may be that God has planted that thought in your mind because He wants you to do something about it!

A story goes that a man was caught in a flood and sitting on his roof. The water kept climbing higher and higher. It was now up to his feet. Just then, someone came by in a canoe, and shouted, "Can I take you to higher ground?"

"No," responded the man, "I have faith in God and He will save me." Soon the water was up to his waist. Just then, someone came along in a motorboat and called out, "Come aboard, and I will take you to where it's safe!"

Again the man refused, "No, I have faith in God and He will save me." Subsequently, a helicopter appeared and the man on the roof had water now up to his neck. "Grab the rope," yelled the pilot from the helicopter. "I'll pull you up." A third time the man refused, saying, "I have faith in God and He will save me." So the helicopter left and the man drowned.

When this fellow arrived in heaven, he was a little put out. In fact, he was indignant. He approached God and complained bitterly. "Tell me," he demanded, "I had faith in You and You let me down! What happened?" "You tell me!" responded God. "I sent you a canoe, a motorboat, and a helicopter, but you refused all three!"[3]

If you need help, in heaven's name, get it! Take it! Receive it! It may be God's way of helping you!

The tendency toward depression is affected by many factors. For instance, our body chemistry can play a part. Our physical condition, our physical well-being, enters in. A lack of regular exercise can be a contributing factor. Inadequate nutrition is another possibility. A lack of pleasure and diversion. "All work and no play" not only can make us dull; it sometimes can make us depressed. So various factors can play a part, and some theorists would develop their entire approach to the matter along one of these lines. Generally, though, there is more to it, and a more comprehensive remedy is required.

But now, at this point, let me suggest four essential steps for licking depression. There is considerable evidence these steps work. Take them—follow them resolutely—and you will get results. You can lick depression! Here they are: Reprogram your mind, soak up the grace of God, set goals and make moves, and develop a positive game plan for every day. Now let's look at these in detail.

First of all, **reprogram your mind.** This is at the heart of what is called "cognitive therapy," an approach used by psychologists and psychiatrists with impressive results. Essentially, depression is a kind of bad habit. It's a habitual way of thinking we've gotten into and have probably been doing for years, very likely from childhood. It's a bad habit of negative thinking turned in upon ourselves. It's a bad habit that has gotten worse and has become acute.

So if we find ourselves depressed, the place to begin is in our customary way of thinking, our own internal conversation, the way our minds have been programmed through the years. Depressed people characteristically put themselves down. They constantly, inwardly, even sometimes outwardly, belittle themselves. They will not permit themselves a strongly unabashed, self-affirming thought.

Dr. David Burns is a progressive and respective psychiatrist who teaches at the University of Pennsylvania School of Medicine. In his excellent book, *Feeling Good: The New Mood Therapy*, he outlines the negative thoughts that do us in. They are, in fact, inaccurate thoughts which we take on face value, or take seriously. As long as they go unchallenged, they set us up for depression. Depressed people think inaccurate thoughts that put them down!

The solution? Learn to recognize faulty thinking, this negative way of seeing things and seeing yourself. Develop techniques of thinking more accurately, more realistically, more positively about yourself. Spot those negative thoughts, and replace them with positive ones. It will take some doing. It may require professional help. There's a large buildup of blurred perception and inaccurate thought. But it can be done, and what a burden is lifted when we succeed!

Take a word of advice from Paul, perhaps the first cognitive therapist, who said, "Whatever things are true, whatever things are noble, whatever things are just, whatever things are pure, whatever things are lovely, whatever things are of good report . . . meditate on these things. . . . and the God of peace will be with you" (Philippians 4:8, 9). Reprogram your mind! Replace all that negativity within!

Second, *soak up the grace of God.* Saturate yourself with the knowledge of the wonderful news of Jesus Christ. Here is the most therapeutic concept in the world! There is nothing more relevant to the essential problem of depression than faith.

What did we say are the two major causes of depression? A loss of confidence in ourselves. A loss of respect for ourselves. We feel powerless and worthless. "I'm no good; I can't do anything right." Okay, so what's the answer?

The beautiful message of Jesus Christ is: "I accept you and love you as you are, and when you take My love and acceptance, from that moment on My worth and power become your worth and power." From then on, that's who you are. From then on, that's what's going for you!

That is, Christ begins actually to live in you! "It is no longer I who live, but Christ lives in me" (Galatians 2:20). That's how Paul described it. Wow! You can't fail! You can't run short! From now on, you have the winning advantage! It's like having a million dollars transferred to your account, and after that, another million, and another, and yet another—so long as you need it! You can never run out!

Now, that doesn't mean you'll never have setbacks. It doesn't mean everything will go easy. It does mean you can't lose! Not with all that going for you! Not with His worth and power turned over to you, so that now it's yours! "I can do all things through Christ who strengthens me" (Philippians 4:13). "Though your sins are like scarlet, they shall be as white as snow" (Isaiah 1:18). Soak up the full reality of the grace of God handed to you through Jesus Christ! Absorb it all! He'll make you feel like a new person! You'll never need to feel down again!

Third, *set goals and make moves.* When you've gotten your thinking straight and you've begun to live amid God's grace showered on you through Christ, then you're ready to set goals—short term and long term. Remember, you can't lose! You're ready to make moves toward the realization of the new and exciting goals. You're ready to take off!

You see, when we get depressed, when we allow negative thoughts to take over, then we surrender to inertia. We get frozen in our tracks. We stay put. We succumb to the paralyzing effects of the status quo. We begin to play it safe. That happens to people, institutions, and churches. What is needed is to set exciting, even daring, goals and then to go for them!

Years ago I preached a sermon on the importance of moving ahead, not losing momentum and surrendering to despair and defeat. Afterwards, a man in his nineties came up to me and said, "You were telling my story! Thirty-five years ago, when I thought I was a great success and well-situated, things happened and suddenly all that was changed. I found myself on the shelf, out of work, out of the running. I went home. I became depressed. I brooded for days on end. I didn't want to live. I was all but finished. Then it hit me: *This will do you no good!* So I started to rethink my situation, to plan a whole new career, even then in my mid-fifties! What followed in the next thirty years was the best part of my life. I was more successful than ever before. I was happier in my work. And a few years ago in my eighties, I retired a happy and fulfilled man." That's the way to do it! Kick depression out the window! Start setting goals! Start making plans! Move ahead!

Fourth, *develop a positive game plan for every day!* Jane Ace, whose dry wit was part of a radio situation-comedy called "Easy Aces" many years ago, often spoke of getting up at "the crank of dawn." Sometimes that's what it takes: a *crank* to get things started. So what! Each day set out to make the most of it. Get vitalized! Get up, get a good breakfast, get going! Take a brisk walk! Spend a few moments in prayer and with Scripture. Decide what you want to do with this one day God has given you. Determine to view the day as a game, a beautiful game, to be played for the joy of it and to be won!

Sometimes, however, on Sunday morning when I wake up I'm not sure how I feel about the morning message I plan to deliver at my church. I may say, "O Lord, it really isn't so hot! I tried to give it my best, but it really isn't so good. I wish I could start over." But of course, I can't. I have to go with it. I have to shake off those negative thoughts. So I get going. I take a shower. I come alive. I get started. And I let God take my poor efforts and turn them into something beautiful for Jesus. It's amazing how He improves that morning message! So get into the game, and win!

Goethe wrote a challenge which has long been a favorite of mine:

> Wouldst thou fashion for thyself a seemly life?
> Then do not fret over what is past and gone;
> And in spite of all thou may'st have left behind
> Live each day as if thy life were just begun.

Never surrender to that demon Depression! Never surrender to Giant Despair! You and I have the tools to win! You and I have the resources to overcome! You and I can lick it! We really can, with God's help!

> We make the world in which we live
> By what we gather and what we give,
> By our daily deeds and the things we say,
> By what we keep or cast away.
>
> We make our world by the beauty we see
> In a skylark's song or a lilac tree.
> In a butterfly's wing, in the pale moon's rise,
> And the wonder that lingers in midnight skies. . . .
>
> We make our world by the goals we pursue,
> By the heights we seek and the higher view,
> By hopes and dreams that reach the sun
> And a will to fight till the heights are won.
>
> ALFRED GRANT WALTON

TWELVE

THE SOLUTION FOR ALL YOUR FEARS

HAVE YOU EVER been afraid, really afraid? Have you ever been terrified, scared out of your skin? Well, I have! That episode remains an unforgettable event in my life. Let me tell you about it.

It was during World War II. I was in the Eighth Air Force then, stationed in England. We were on our second or third bombing mission over Germany and well into enemy territory. Our B–17 "Flying Fortress" was flying at an altitude of twenty thousand feet or more. Suddenly there came over the intercom these petrifying words: "Flak at three o'clock!"

"Flak?" said I. I had had no advance warning of flak, the normal procedure during a mission. "Did we have an alert on this?" I yelled, quickly getting on the intercom. "Yes," came the answer, "twenty minutes ago!" "Twenty minutes ago!" I shouted in desperation. "I didn't hear it!"

103

Apparently when the alert was given, I was on another channel, handling the radio, so I didn't get the message. Now flak was exploding all around us, and I had no flak suit on! I was dangerously exposed to whatever pieces of steel might come flying through our plane. Frantically, I struggled to get the suit on—a heavy cape filled with overlapping steel scales. It weighed a ton. For all my struggles, in my panic I could not get it on. Putting on a flak suit requires a careful, deliberate, methodical technique, and just then my technique was all shot. I couldn't have been more clumsy. I had visions of flak piercing my body at any moment, hitting my heart, puncturing my lungs, my throat, my brain. It would be "curtains"!

Then I realized I had to get control of myself. All this fear would do me no good. At this rate, I would never get the suit on. An inner voice said, "Morgan, calm down! You're letting yourself get carried away! Control your panic! Control your fear!" So, by sheer willpower, I stopped the frenzy, began to breathe in a calm and controlled way, and put out of my mind all sense of danger. Now I was in charge of myself and succeeded in getting the flak suit on as well as the heavy steel helmet. I had conquered my fear!

Now, of course, that was an unusual situation, one I would never want to repeat, but it illustrates something. It illustrates what happens when we allow fear to take over. Many people are frequently as much at the mercy of their fears as I was that day during World War II. When that happens, they are incapacitated. They become inept. They lose effectiveness. If there's anything we need to know if we're going to get it together, it's how to deal with our fears, how to manage them, how to control them.

What's the answer? What's the solution? One of the best statements ever made on this was by Paul in his second letter to his young friend, Timothy. It's a fantastic passage. Anybody could go back to it again and again and get enormous benefit from it. Drench your mind in it. In chapter 1, verse 7, Paul says, "For God has not given us a spirit of fear, but of power and of love and of a sound mind." Now, what's that mean? This—God doesn't want us fearful! God doesn't want us fear-driven and fear-ridden! God wants us on top of our fears! How? By power and love and a sound mind!

Now, let's look at those words, except let me reverse their order. Paul began with power, then he spoke of love, and finally a sound mind. I want to work it the other way around: first, a sound mind; then, love; and finally, power!

First, a sound mind—**keep your mind sound!** We need that! I remember reading of how an English bishop put it a few centuries ago when commenting on the clergy in his diocese. He said some had gone out of their minds, others were going out of their minds, and a good many had no minds to go out of! So, a sound mind is important! And there are four suggestions for keeping your mind sound.

1. *Monitor your mind.* Keep an eye on it. Notice what's going on there! Be alert to subtle shifts. Oversee the operation. Don't allow your mind to play tricks on you. Monitor it. Keep tabs on what you're thinking about.

2. *Moderate your mind.* Keep the critical balance. One of the best books ever written on the human mind is *The Vital Balance* by America's foremost psychiatrist, Dr. Karl Menninger. Dr. Menninger describes how people become neurotic or even psychotic. He says the mind is like a ship on the high seas. Storms and winds will assail it, but ballast keeps it upright. Correctives are going on all the time, maintaining the vital balance. So with our minds: We need to keep alert to those influences and attitudes

which can gradually tilt us too far until our balance of outlook is lost. Keep mentally upright! Keep the vital balance!

All sorts of things can throw us off, cause us to lean too far this way or that. Self-pity is one. We can't afford the luxury of self-pity, no matter what. It's always damaging. It's a negative, self-centered response to life's difficulties. Anger is another. We've seen what anger can do. It's poison! "Do not let the sun go down on your wrath," is God's directive (Ephesians 4:26). Corruption is another. Watch out for corrupting influences. We live in a world filled with them, but we must not allow them to cling to our lives, invade our minds, and flood our consciousness. They are like barnacles on a ship; in time they will drag us down by sheer weight. Scrape them off, and remember, we have a positive remedy for them. It's the Lordship of Jesus Christ who redeems us, cleanses us, restores us, and recreates us. But to allow corruption to go unchecked and unchallenged in our lives will slowly tip the ship and sink it! It's not the way to a sound mind. Here's another attitude to watch out for: paranoia—being suspicious or of a suspicious nature. It's taking things personally, always feeling people are against you. This, in turn, can lead to a martyr complex. That makes us all the more fearful and fear-prone. So watch out for paranoia. It's unhealthy, it's destructive, and it's wrong. People really aren't thinking that much about us anyway, you know. They're generally thinking about themselves! Always keep the "vital balance" of a healthy mind. Moderate it.

3. *Manage it.* That's the beautiful thing about being created in the image of God, as Scripture puts it. That means we have a mind and we can use it. We have a control center. We can decide what we'll think about. We

can decide how that mind will be occupied. We've looked at the importance of positively programming our minds, and Paul has given us a whole series of positive mental exercises for that in Philippians 4:8, 9 so you can learn how to manage your mind!

4. *Maximize it.* Put it on the fast track. Put it on the high road. Pace your mind by the One whose mind is the most beautiful and positive of all. Think along with Him. "Let this mind be in you which was also in Christ Jesus" (Philippians 2:5). That's healthy! That's wholesome! That's headed somewhere!

So, throughout life, maintain a sound mind. That's one of the best ways to protect ourselves from fear and fearfulness. There is a poem which, in its own way, expresses this. It's one of my favorites. It appears on a wall at the beautiful cathedral at Chester, England.

> Give me a good digestion, Lord,
> And also something to digest.
> Give me a healthy body, Lord,
> With sense to keep it at its best.
>
> Give me a healthy mind, good Lord,
> To keep the good and pure in sight,
> Which, seeing sin, is not appalled
> But finds a way to set it right.
>
> Give me a mind that is not bored,
> That does not whimper, whine, or sigh;
> Don't let me worry overmuch
> About the fussy thing called "I."
>
> Give me a sense of humor, Lord.
> Give me the grace to see a joke,
> To get some pleasure out of life
> And pass it on to other folk.

"For God has not given us a spirit of fear, but of power and of love and of a sound mind."

Second in our sequence is love—*let love flow through your life!* Love will overcome fear. An eminent psychiatrist, Dr. Gerald G. Jampolsky, says the opposite of love is not hate. No, the opposite of love is fear. That means, to overcome fear, fill your life with love. Let love become the dominant force in your life. First John 4:18: "There is no fear in love; but perfect love casts out fear. . . ." What does that suggest? Resolve to approach all people in a spirit of love, for love conquers all.

Love in your heart frees you from fear; relates you to the Source of Life, God; and releases positive feelings to overcome hostility, redress wrongs, heal hurts, and build relationships. Love is the strongest force in the world. It's what "makes the world go 'round." It gives you the winning advantage in all human contacts. "There is no fear in love; but perfect love casts out fear."

Remember the words of Edwin Markham in "Outwitted"? Think of the enormous power of love as expressed in his poem:

> He drew a circle that shut me out—
> Heretic, rebel, a thing to flout.
> But love and I had the wit to win:
> We drew a circle that took him in!

"For God has not given us a spirit of fear, but of power and of love and of a sound mind."

And the third, power—*take the power in!* Much of the fear people experience is because they feel powerless. They feel themselves at the mercy of things or forces beyond their control. This causes them to cower before life.

It renders them ineffectual and incapacitated. And they are soon defeated!

But who says they are powerless? If you *say* you are, then, of course, you will be. This is self-fulfilling prophecy. In studies on the depressed, it's been found they generally hold themselves at fault for whatever goes wrong while at the same time they feel powerless against the forces around them. There is a kind of contradiction here: to be the prime cause but equally to be incapable of causing anything. It's hard to have it both ways! Obviously, this is an example of distorted reality. It's simply not true!

You are not powerless, nor are you responsible for everything that happens. Some things are quite out of your hands. They may be somebody else's business, and you have to accept that. But many things are quite within the realm of your powerful response. You can make a difference there. Why? Because God made you powerful and God will make you more powerful.

For one thing, to be a human being at all is to be fearfully and wonderfully made. As a human being, you are at the very pinnacle of creation. You have been equipped with capacities you will never fully exhaust. There is always more you can do, a greater and stronger response you can make, a more creative and effective approach you can attempt. You are a power center because you are created in the image of God!

But beyond that, to be a child of God, redeemed by Jesus Christ, makes you more than a conquerer. Paul says that: "Yet in all these things we are more than conquerors through Him who loved us" (Romans 8:37). How is that? Have you ever noticed how often the word *power* appears in the New Testament? Do you remember how Jesus said He would send the Holy Spirit and that would mean power for the lives of the disciples? If there is anything we believers can believe in, it's that Higher and Greater Power who helps us, the very Power at the heart of the universe, the Power of God! When, through Jesus Christ, your Lord and Savior, you give yourself to God, in no time at all you are in the power of the Spirit. And then, in the forceful words of 1 John 4:4: "He who is in you is greater than he who is in the world."

The solution for our fears? It is living and breathing this truth until the reality of it takes form in us and we become "more than conquerors through Him who loved us." "For," we are wonderfully assured, "God has not given us a spirit of fear, but of power and of love and of a sound mind."

Let me conclude this with inspiring words with which you and I might begin every day. They are the exceptionally beautiful words of a truly Spirit-filled man, Albert W. Palmer. Try using them every morning, and see if they don't fill your entire day with a sense of the presence and power of God who overcomes all fear.

All this day I am going to be a child of God. His love is round about me. Underneath are the everlasting arms. I am going to be honest and true in all events of life and I believe that to those who love God all things work together for good. I am going to rise above worry, fretting, fear and hatred, and live in an atmosphere of spiritual serenity. Behind all that comes, God's love and wisdom will be present to strengthen and sustain.

THIRTEEN

YOU'RE AS YOUNG AS YOUR DREAMS!

SOME OF US can remember a song from yesterday: "When I Grow Too Old to Dream." Maybe you remember it. Maybe you can hum it or sing it. The lyrics raise interesting questions. For instance, what is it to grow old? What is it to stay young? Why do some people get old so quickly? Why do others retain a youthful spirit? I've thought a lot about this through the years, and I have a suggestion: You're as young as your dreams! You really are!

I've known some people of advanced years who were very youthful, and I've known some in the spring of life who were very, very old. I remember some people saying of a woman at the time of her death, "Why, she was old when she was a little girl!" What makes the difference? Why are some people over the hill so soon? Somebody said, "When you're over the hill, you pick up speed." You sure do! You're headed for the bottom! Why do others never seem to be over the hill? "When I Grow Too Old to

Dream''—is that the clue? Is that the connection? You're as old as your dreams!

The prophet Joel said a long time ago, ''Your old men shall dream dreams, Your young men shall see visions'' (Joel 2:28). My friend Bruce Larson has been called a visionary. I think he is. Maybe that's why he always seems so youthful, so young! I do believe there is a connection, and I do believe if we can see the connection, we can keep young in mind and heart and, yes, even in body.

Someone in modern times wrote, ''Youth is not a time of life. . . . It is a state of mind. Nobody grows old by merely living a number of years; people grow old by deserting their ideals. Years wrinkle the skin, but to give up enthusiasm wrinkles the soul. Worry, doubt, self-distrust, fear, and despair—these are the long years that bow the head and turn the growing spirit back to dust. . . . You are as young as your faith, as old as your doubt; as young as your self-confidence, as old as your fear; as young as your hope, as old as your despair.'' And I'm going to add because I really believe it—you are as young as your dreams!

We need dreams! We need visions! They turn us on! They call us forth, call us out, call us on. We even need fantasies, don't we? Three men went on a fishing trip. Their boat was wrecked in a storm, but they managed to swim to a desert island. For the first few days all was well. But after a week, one of the three, a cattle baron, became despondent; he missed his ranch. A second longed for his native Manhattan, where he was a cab driver. The third man, a happy-go-lucky type, was enjoying himself, finding the experience rather peaceful. One day, as they were walking along the beach, the carefree fellow happened to see an ancient lamp which he promptly picked up. Then he rubbed it and a genie sprang out. "For freeing me from my prison," said the genie, "each of you shall receive *one* wish." "I'd like to be back on my ranch," said the cattle baron, quick to grab the opportunity. *Poof!* He was gone! "I'd like to be driving my hack again," said the cabby, also unwilling to let this chance pass him by. *Poof!* He was gone! "And what is your wish?" asked the genie of the third man, who by then was looking a little forlorn. "Well," he said, "I'm kinda lonely now without the other guys. I wish they were back." *Poof! Poof!*

Ah, yes, but we're not talking whimsy. We're talking reality. And the reality is that some of us grow old and some of us stay young. Some of us are old before our time, and some of us never seem to age at all. "When I Grow Too Old to Dream"? That's the problem! That's the hitch! They've stopped dreaming, or they never dreamed at all! We grow old when we stop dreaming or because we never allowed ourselves to have dreams. You're as *young* as your dreams!

The study of aging is a fascinating subject. The process of aging is under constant study these days. They're learning amazing things. It remains a mystery, but old myths are giving way to new understanding. Assumptions long held are giving way to facts, and what we're learning ought to encourage us all. We can remain young for a lot longer than we thought!

You see—and this is the really exciting thing—aging seems to have more to do with stimulation or the lack of it. Except in the case of disease, aging seems to have more to do with exciting interests or the lack of them. Aging seems to have more to do with great dreams, wonderful plans, and challenging hopes or the lack of them. You wouldn't expect me to quote Mae West, I suppose, but I can't resist. She was onto something when she said as one of her famous lines, "It's not the men in my life, but the life in my men."

I heard a psychiatrist lecturing on aging several years ago. He was a specialist in geriatrics. He noted that findings do not indicate people age gradually, as a steady and inevitable process, but sporadically, in spurts. Today they're in one condition; tomorrow they're in quite another condition. These spurts, these sudden declines, seem related to events or the lack of events in their lives. In other words, external factors, not internal—certainly not an automatic aging process. Aging seems to be associated with a change of spirit, a change of outlook, a change of attitude. If you give up and lie low, you get old. If you get up and get going, you keep young. You and I need—and thrive on—challenging interests, exciting opportunities, and wonderful dreams. That's the key to staying young. "When I Grow Too Old to Dream"? That's the point—you're as young as your dreams!

There's something more here. Our mental powers do not necessarily decline with age. That's a myth. We know that because the evidence is coming in fast! Years ago I spent a year studying intelligence and the measurement of intelligence. I was trained to test people, and I did—in schools, in hospitals, and privately. We were taught a lot of things about intelligence—assumptions that are not holding up very well these days. It's really exciting to see it all get turned around!

For example, recent studies of human intelligence suggest that much of the assumed decline (we were taught a person declines by 10 percent every ten years after thirty!) is due to faulty testing or to self-fulfilling prophecy. Tests used in the past were geared to the young; therefore, the young did better and the older people didn't fare so well. This skewed everything and led to false conclusions.

Also, people expecting to decline (they had been *told* they would), anticipating it, almost counting on it, tended to give up! They let it happen. They quietly ceased making the effort to keep alive, alert, growing in knowledge and skills. They stopped using their muscles, and so the muscles atrophied. They stopped challenging their minds with new ideas and new skills, and so their minds became sluggish. I am more and more convinced we should think of our minds the way we think of our muscles: Use them or lose them! This proves our point: You're as young as your dreams!

Here's something else to think about:

> We are all of us dreamers of dreams,
>   On visions our childhood is fed;
> And the heart of the child is unhaunted, it seems,
>   By the ghosts of dreams that are dead.
>
> From childhood to youth's but a span,
>   And the years of our life are soon sped;
> But the youth is no longer a youth, but a man,
>   When the first of his dreams is dead.
>
> 'Tis a cup of wormwood and gall,
>   When the doom of a great dream is said;
> But the best of a man is under the pall,
>   When the best of his dreams is dead.
>
> He may live on by compact and plan,
>   When the fine bloom of living is shed;
> But God pity the little that's left of a man
>   When the last of his dreams is dead.

Let him show a brave face if he can,
  Let him woo fame or fortune instead;
Yet there's not much to do but to bury a man,
  When the last of his dreams is dead.

                    WILLIAM HERBERT CARRUTH

Conclusion? Whatever your age in terms of years, you're as young as your dreams!

My father lived to be ninety-two. He retired when he was eighty-four, taking early retirement! He kept alive his dreams, and I helped him. When he was seventy-five, I realized he hadn't traveled much. He had always kept busy with his architecture. So I tried to open up for him a whole new vista of life. I said, "Pop, why don't you take a trip around the world?" Wow! That all but floored him! He resisted the suggestion at first, but then we reached a compromise. He would take a trip to the Caribbean. Once he made up his mind, once the idea caught hold, he was excited. He began to make plans. He read up on the region and prepared to make the most of it. He went and had a glorious time.

Soon after he got back, I said to him, "Pop, where next?"

"I just got back!" he responded.

"I know," I persisted, "but you've got to start looking ahead to the next trip!" So he relented, and decided on Bermuda. Again, he got excited. Again, he had a glorious time. Upon his return, I prodded him again. Well, he'd go to Hawaii. So he did, and after that he would head for Europe. He had always wanted to visit the Mediterranean, Greece, Italy—the source of so much of the architecture and art to which he had devoted his life. But, unfortunately, that was not to be. For reasons of health, that fourth trip never took place.

Nonetheless, my father lived to be ninety-two. I am

convinced that having those plans, those goals, those
dreams helped to keep him young. They prolonged his
life! You see, you're as young as your dreams, whatever
they are!

What happens when you have dreams? Dreams set in
motion a life-producing succession of motivating events:

> Dreams evoke plans.
> Plans evoke effort.
> Effort evokes energy.
> Energy evokes strength.
> Strength evokes life!

You come alive, you stay alive, you keep alive, because
of your dreams!

First, dreams evoke plans. You begin thinking about
possibilities, how you might do it, what it would take,
how it could be accomplished. The mind gets turned on.

Pretty soon, you're developing plans. You turn it over
in your mind, and come up with schemes for doing it.

When you have a plan, right away you're seeing how
simple it is after all. It really can be done, and you're
beginning to see how you might do it. The plan suggests
the order of events, what the first, second, and third steps
might be. Plans are appealing.

Now you feel like making the effort. You take a step,
and one step calls forth a second step, and so on and so
forth. It's like walking—as soon as you've taken one step,
you're off balance and you're poised to take the second
step. Already you're moving; it's beginning to happen.

When you make the effort, you discover energy welling
up within you. It's energy you probably didn't know you
had, not, at least, when you were practically dormant with

inactivity. Sleep produces sleep, inactivity produces inactivity, inertia produces inertia, and so on. But effort elicits strength. It was there, waiting to be used, waiting to be turned on!

When you release energy, you gain strength. You feel physically stronger, and you feel psychologically and spiritually invigorated. You are stronger than you ever imagined. It's coming forth! It's happening! Strength is being drawn out of you!

And when strength comes, you feel alive. You feel well. You're doing what you should be doing, living as you should be living. You're fulfilling what God had in mind for you when He equipped you with all sorts of amazing capacities. "Those who wait on the Lord" receive His inspiration, beautiful dreams, glorious visions. And so, they "shall renew their strength; They shall mount up with wings like eagles, They shall run and not be weary, They shall walk and not faint" (Isaiah 40:31).

When you grow too old to dream? Oh, no! Say instead, you're as young as your dreams! "I have come that they may have life" (John 10:10). You're as young as your dreams!

> What would we do in this world of ours
>   Were it not for the dreams ahead?
> For thorns are mixed with the blooming flowers
>   No matter which path we tread.
>
> And each of us has his golden goal,
>   Stretching far into the years;
> And ever he climbs with a hopeful soul,
>   With alternate smiles and tears.
>
> That dream ahead is what holds him up
>   Through the storms of a ceaseless fight;
> When his lips are pressed to the wormwood's cup
>   And clouds shut out the light.

To some it's a dream of high estate;
  To some it's a dream of wealth;
To some it's a dream of a truce with Fate
  In a constant search for health.

To some it's a dream of home and wife;
  To some it's a crown above;
The dreams ahead are what make each life—
  The dreams—and faith—and love!

EDWIN CARLILE LITSEY

FOURTEEN

THE ART OF KEEPING YOUR COOL

ONE DAY, MANY long years ago, when I was an airman in the Army Air Force and preparing to go overseas and into combat, I lay on my bunk reading a book. Suddenly my eyes were frozen on one of the most compelling statements I had ever read. I was only twenty at the time, but I was enthralled by Ralph Waldo Emerson's essay on "Self-Reliance." The words that caught my attention I have never forgotten.

This is what Emerson wrote: "It is easy in the world to live after the world's opinions; it is easy in solitude to live after our own; but the great man is he who in the midst of the crowd keeps with perfect sweetness the independence of solitude."

Is there a more valuable quality of life, a more needed state of being? "The world is too much with us," we say. The strident demands of society bombard us from all directions. We live amid incessant noise, a whirl of activity, discordant claims, a cacophony of opinions. If there is anything we need, it is this extraordinary quality, this enviable state, which Emerson so deeply etched in my mind long ago—this poise, this sense of solitude amid the crowd, this composure.

We have seen how Jesus kept His cool, how He maintained His composure. It was while He was visiting Nazareth, among the dear people "who knew Him when." But they tried to do Him in. They not only resented what He had to say during His short talk in the synagogue; they made an effort to take His life. They hustled Him off to the edge of town, to a high cliff, with the clear intention of pushing this Son of theirs to His death. How did the Master react? What did He do? He simply kept His cool and walked calmly through the crowd. With extraordinary presence of mind and composure, He went His way. Here's how Luke reports that remarkable incident: "Then passing through the midst of them, He went His way" (Luke 4:30). That's class! That's composure!

What Emerson has so unforgettably portrayed and Jesus has so gloriously modeled, Rudyard Kipling set to verse in this familiar poem:

> If you can keep your head when all about you
>   Are losing theirs and blaming it on you,
> If you can trust yourself when all men doubt you,
>   But make allowance for their doubting too;
> If you can wait and not be tired of waiting,
>   Or be lied about, don't deal in lies,
> Or being hated don't give way to hating,
>   And yet don't look too good, nor talk too wise. . . .
>
> Yours is the Earth and everything that's in it,
>   And—which is more—you'll be a Man, my son!

An enviable quality? You bet! A necessary style in to-day's world? No doubt about it! It may be the one quality we today most need to cultivate, more than any other, if we're to hold ourselves together and rise above the frenzy and passions of the times. But how? How do you keep your poise, your sense of solitude amid the crowd, your composure? As I see it, and as I have concluded after a lot of reflection since that day when lying on my bunk I read "Self-Reliance," there are five essentials for keeping your composure in the midst of it all.

The first is this: ***Don't expect too much of other people.*** Don't build yourself up for a big letdown. Don't set the stage for shattering disillusionment where people are con-cerned. How can a person of faith avoid disillusionment? By having no illusions! By understanding something about human frailty and sin. Obviously Jesus understood this. He was the most realistic Person who ever lived so far as human nature was concerned. He loved people. He had high hopes for them. He was ready to die for them, in fact. But He also "knew what was in Man." He was no fuzzy-headed romantic. He knew a thing or two about human nature and the way people react. He knew enough not to expect too much. Even when confronted with hostility and threats to His life, He did not fall apart. He kept His poise. He kept His cool. He kept His composure.

You see, people, even those near and dear to us, will not always do and say what we want, or agree with our opinions, or accept what we have to offer. They have their funny ways, too. Those who depend upon others always coming through as they had hoped set themselves up for a tremendous letdown. No, people have their own agenda. You can try to persuade them, you can try to enlist them, you can try to make them understand—but don't count on their coming through every time. Don't expect too much of other people.

One of my heroes is Sir William Osler, the wise and celebrated physician of yesteryear. My father-in-law, a physician himself and one of the finest men I ever knew, used to quote Osler. He knew him chapter and verse. I'm sure he was aware of this statement by the great man: "One way to gain imperturbability is not to expect too much from the people amongst whom you dwell. In matters medical, the average citizen today has not one whit more sense than the Romans of long ago. Deal gently, therefore, with this deliciously credulous human nature! Restrain your indignation when you find your pet parson carrying a bottle of sugar pills in his pocket, or when you accidentally discover a case of patent medicine in the bedroom of your best patient. It must needs be that offenses of this kind come. Expect them, and do not be vexed by them."

The second essential for keeping your composure is this: **Don't expect too much of yourself.** If you need to understand how others tick, you need to understand how *you* tick, too. If you need to acquire patience for others and their "deliciously" (Osler's word) human ways, you need patience with yourself, also. Which is to say, don't saddle yourself with perfectionistic demands. The only One to whom perfection has ever been attributed was Jesus, and you wouldn't want to crowd Him now, would you? Perfectionism misses the point of the Gospel, the Good News, that none of us is perfect and all of us need to lean heavily on divine grace. In other words, don't organize your life or arrange your expectations for inevitable disappointment and failure. You'll never be a winner that way!

People have all sorts of ways of putting themselves at a disadvantage, putting themselves over a barrel. Maybe they over-schedule their day or their week. Or maybe they allow others to over-schedule for them. No way can they accomplish all these things within the alloted time! So they spend their entire day under excessive pressure, never quite on top of things, never quite on schedule, and with the added burden of concluding the day with a sense of failure and defeat. No, we need spaces in our schedules. We need allowances for the unpredictable, if we're to work efficiently and effectively, if we're to maintain our peace and poise and composure.

Maybe we expect too much in our accomplishments, wanting to write Beethoven's "Ninth Symphony" when we ought to be satisfied with having written Debussy's "Clair de Lune" (assuming we're Debussy, of course!). See what then happens. When we hold out to ourselves the challenge of doing something we cannot do, something beyond our capacity, something out of character, we then set ourselves up for failure and a feeling of worthlessness. It's all due to false, excessive expectations. We miss out on doing what we can do, what maybe we alone could do. We set in motion negative feelings that impede our greatest creativity.

Let me tell you what I do when I'm inclined to expect too much of myself—I simply remember Ted Williams. He was one of the greatest baseball players of all time. Today he is honored in the Baseball Hall of Fame in Cooperstown, New York. I remember his hitting those stunning home runs out of Fenway Park. But I also remember he never hit much better than .400! He didn't hit 1.000, which would have been perfect. He didn't hit .800. He didn't even hit .500! More often than not, he didn't connect at all! Ted Williams only batted a little better than .400, but .400

is about the best in baseball history! The point? Strive to be your best; set worthy goals—but don't fall into the trap of perfectionism. That's one thing we as believers don't need to get into. We've been saved from that. Don't expect too much of yourself!

The third essential for keeping your composure is this: *Focus on the present.* It's an old rule, but it's a good rule. Sometimes it's called "living in day-tight compartments." What it means is this. Avoid scattering your attention, your energy, and your power. Keep your eye on the target. Focus on the present. Concentrate on what you're doing now—today—this very hour—this very minute. Bar the rude intrusion of distracting thoughts and upsetting worries.

Our little friend Charlie Brown in the comic strip "Peanuts" had the idea. "I've developed a new philosophy," he said. "I only dread one day at a time."

It's what our Lord was getting at when He said in the Sermon on the Mount, "Do not worry about tomorrow, for tomorrow will worry about its own things. Sufficient for the day is its own trouble" (Matthew 6:34).

Focus on the present. Bring everything you've got to this. If you're working, work. If you're praying, pray. If you're relaxing, relax. Bring penetrating concentration to the present. This means screening out the past—the past cannot be changed. It means avoiding reliving everything that ever went wrong. Focus on the present! It also means controlling the impulse to dwell too much in the future. Some forward-looking is necessary, in order to make good plans. But don't take up premature residence there. I remember seeing a placard somewhere which read: "Why worry about tomorrow? We may not make it through today." Live in the present!

Robert Louis Stevenson made one of the finest statements on this: "Anyone can carry his burden, however hard, until nightfall. Anyone can live serenely, patiently, lovingly, purely, till the sun goes down. And this is all that life really means."

Focus on the present!

The fourth essential is this: *Commit everything to God.* Whatever you're doing, whatever you're trying to do, leave the results to Him. Leave to God the issue of your hopes, your struggles, your dreams. Never mind the results! Never mind how it all adds up! Do what you have to do and do it with all your might, but then let it go. Let it float off into His eternal purposes.

Of course, this means guarding against a rigid predetermination or premature judgment as to how things ought to come out. Leave room for God to "fudge it" a little, bring it out a little differently and probably a whole lot better. Yield your plans to His master plan, and trust Him to bring it along wonderfully.

Have you ever wondered what Paul had in mind when he said, "All things work together for good to those who love God" (Romans 8:28)? I think he was saying we can safely leave the results to Him, that there is a master strategy which neither you nor I can decipher just now. Phillips' translation captures this, I think: "We know that to those who love God, who are called according to his plan, everything that happens fits into a pattern for good." You see, He's got a plan. It may not be yours; it may not be mine. But He's got a plan. If we simply do our best, keep working, commit all our efforts to Him, it will all come out. It will all come together. You'll get it together!

It was the darkest hour for Britain during World War II, at the time of the fierce bombings of London and the Battle of Dunkirk, when Leslie Weatherhead wrote this inspiring message to his fellow Britons: "God will win whether we win or lose. So in God, if we remain loyal to Him, the victory will be ours, even if it looks like defeat and is called defeat and feels like defeat. The cross felt like defeat to Jesus and it looked like defeat to His disciples and was called defeat by the world. Yet it was God's greatest victory. Let us then prepare for victory, be worthy of it, and know how to apply it for God's purposes."

Commit everything to God!

Finally, there is this: *Live with an eternal view.* From day to day, keep before you an eternal vista, for it will broaden your spirit and enlarge your soul. Jefferson drew inspiration from his vista at Monticello. He needed it. Churchill surrounded himself with the broad and gracious vistas of Chartwell, his country home southeast of London where he wrote all his books. When you see it, you realize why there is grandeur of spirit and thought running through everything Churchill wrote. He caught it, or kept it alive, at Chartwell. Spaciousness without has a way of evoking spaciousness within!

So live with an eternal view. When you have it, you're less likely to fret or fidget. You're more likely to be at peace, to be serene and tranquil. It's like the widow in Vermont who lost her home by fire. Her neighbors decided to band together and build her a house, and so asked her what changes she would like in her new home which was to be modeled after the old one. She thought about this for a while, and then she said, "I'll tell you what—I'd just love to have a window over my kitchen sink."

There you have it! What more is there to say? The essentials for keeping your composure? Don't expect too much from other people. Don't expect too much of yourself. Focus on the present. Commit everything to God. And this—live with an eternal view! Have a window over your kitchen sink!

FIFTEEN

PAY THE TOLL TO REACH THE GOAL!

THE TOLL BOOTHS have come down in Connecticut! It created quite a stir in our state for a while. Lots of people, I noticed, were pleased with this gratuitous development. Along the interstates and over the bridges the booths were removed, at least at many locations. When passing over the Connecticut River by means of the Putnam Bridge that connects our town of Wethersfield with the neighboring town of Glastonbury, I no longer need to stop and pay the toll. It's now free passage all the way.

But is it? You mean there are no costs? There are no expenses? It's literally free? I doubt it. We do pay. Make no mistake about it, we pay! It's only that we don't pay at the toll booths. But, while there may be advantages and sound reasons for the elimination of the booths, I've wondered how good it is to have this illusion that you can have free rides over the highways and bridges of our state. Because,

you see, there are no free rides—not anywhere, not in Glastonbury, not even to heaven. There is a price. There are costs, and sooner or later, we have to accept them.

It's funny, isn't it, how we shrink from the costs? It's funny how, when we see the price tag, we pull back! Then we say it's more than we bargained for. I love the story of the small boy in school who told his classmates he wanted to be a doctor. Then his teacher said, "What would you do if I came to you with a tummy ache?"

"I don't know," said the boy.

"What would you do if I had a broken arm?"

Again, the boy said, "I don't know." Then, after a moment's reflection, the lad added, "Maybe I'd better be a lawyer."[4] When he saw what was involved, he pulled back!

Sometimes I've thought to myself that perhaps our Lord Jesus might have done the same. At any number of points during His ministry on earth, He might have said, "Forget it!" But early on, He saw the price that had to be paid. He saw the costs that had to be accepted. Isn't that what He was trying to get across to Peter that day at Philippi? Remember, when Peter had just made the most important statement of his life? "You are the Christ," he proclaimed gloriously, "the Son of the living God" (Matthew 16:16).

Then Jesus went on to explain what that meant, what it would cost—that He, Jesus, "must go to Jerusalem, and suffer many things . . . and be killed. . . ." Peter protested. It didn't fit his neat and painless picture of the Messiah. So he said, "Far be it from You, Lord; this shall not happen to You!" It was Peter's way of saying, "Is this trip necessary?" And Jesus responded angrily, "Get behind Me, Satan! You are an offense to Me. . . ." He was saying, in effect, "A moment ago you made the most

beautiful statement of your life, but now you speak for the devil himself. So soon have you come down to this!?'' Then Jesus expanded on what He had been saying. "If anyone desires to come after Me, let him deny himself, and take up his cross, and follow Me. For whoever desires to save his life will lose it, and whoever loses his life for My sake will find it" (Matthew 16:21–25).

The point? There's a price, and we have to pay it. There are costs, and we have to accept them. If there is a phrase that captures the message and leaves no doubt, none whatever, of what we need to understand, it is this: *Pay the toll to reach the goal!*

No, there's a strong inclination to shrink from this reality, the way comedian Flip Wilson's imagined congregation shrank from it. On a Bob Hope show a while back, Wilson was impersonating a preacher. While working into his sermon one Sunday, the preacher said, "If this church is going to progress, it's got to crawl, it's got to crawl!"

At once, the congregation, getting into the spirit of the message, responded, "Make it crawl, Rev! Make it crawl!"

Then the preacher said, "And if this church is going to progress, it's got to stand, it's got to stand!"

Again the congregation responded enthusiastically, "Make it stand, Rev! Make it stand!"

Then the preacher said, "And if this church is going to progress, it's got to run, it's got to run!"

Again the congregation shouted in agreement, "Make it run, Rev! Make it run!"

Then the preacher said, "If this church is going to progress, it's got to give, it's got to give!"

But this time the congregation answered, "Make it *crawl*, Rev! Make it *crawl!*"

They didn't want to pay the price. They didn't want to

accept the costs! But Jesus says there's a cross to be borne, there's a price to be paid. You have to *pay the toll to reach the goal!*

What if Jesus had backed off? What if He had decided not to go to Jerusalem, not to take on the political and ecclesiastical powers, not to get into that big flap? What if He had said, "This is too much! This is more than anyone should endure!"? What if there had never been the Last Supper, the arrest, the trial, or the Crucifixion? What if all that had never happened because Jesus had decided the cost was too much? There are, by the way, religious groups, pseudo-Christian sects, which would eliminate these harsher shades of the Christian story and reduce the significance of the Cross.

No, Jesus could have called it a day at several points: in Gethsemane, as He prayed, "O My Father, . . . let this cup pass from Me; nevertheless, not as I will, but as You will" (Matthew 26:39). Or before Pilate, as the Roman ruler said, in effect, "Have you nothing to say in Your defense?" (*See* Matthew 27:13.) Or even, at the last, on the Cross, as the crowd taunted Him unmercifully, saying, "If You are the Son of God, come down from the cross!" (Matthew 27:40.) Of course, if He had, there would have been no Easter Morn. Equally, there would have been no Christian faith founded upon the Crucifixion and the Resurrection. He paid the price, this Jesus! He accepted the cost! He did it because, as He understood, you have to *pay the toll to reach the goal!*

This applies to everything, doesn't it? Whatever we set out to do, whatever we set out to be, there is a cost. There is no free passage. There is no instant gratification. Do you want to achieve something as a human being? Do you want to see your life develop? If you're a young person, do you want to make headway in school or in some activity or in a sport? Or, later on, do you want to make something of yourself, have a fine career, or do something worthwhile for the world? If you are older, do you want to attain new heights professionally or personally? Or do you want to learn a new skill, get started in a new field, or come by some new understanding or knowledge? Then remember—there's a price!

Here in our land, we want to see our nation move ahead and be more than it's ever been. Or in the Christian faith today, we want to see the Church fulfilling all that God would have it be. Then remember, there's a price! Whatever the undertaking, you have to *pay the toll to reach the goal!*

Jesus said, "Take up your cross and follow Me." A lot of people, it seems to me, misunderstood Jesus on this. There is a tendency to trivialize His meaning. Someone suffers a hardship, a critical ailment, a great loss, and says too soon, too glibly, "Oh, that's my cross!" But it isn't! Not by a long shot! Our cross is never something we endure against our will or without choice. It's never something imposed upon us, over which we have no control. No, our cross is something we knowingly and willingly accept for a higher purpose, a higher good, a higher calling. It's a price we agree to pay. We can reject it, even as Jesus could have rejected His. We can refuse it, even as Jesus had ample opportunity to refuse His. We can turn it down, saying, "No, I won't do it!" Notice that the wording is, "*Take up* your cross. . . ." That's voluntary. It's something we choose to do. Bearing your cross is paying the price, paying the toll, for whatever it is upon which you place your highest value—perhaps whatever it is you worship.

Years ago I came upon a passage in the writings of William James, America's great psychologist of many decades ago. I can't tell you how many times I've thought about his statement through the years. This is what James wrote: "Let no youth have any anxiety about the upshot of his education, whatever the line of it may be. If he keeps faithfully busy every hour of the working day, he may safely leave the final result to itself. He can with perfect certainty count on waking up some fine morning to find himself one of the competent ones of his generation, in whatever pursuit he may have singled out." What is that in other words? *Pay the toll to reach the goal!*

In the life of faith the same is true. You get out of it what you put into it. There is a cross to be borne. There is a price to be paid. Charles Colson, in his little book with the subtitle *How to Evangelize Our Self-Centered Culture*, points to the great disparity these days between professions of faith and actual performance. Ninety-five percent of Americans claim to believe in God. More than 50 million Americans claim to be "born again." Then why, Colson wants to know, do they not make a greater impact upon our society? Why do not more lives show the telling force of Jesus Christ? "The answer," suggests Colson, "is what Dietrich Bonhoeffer, the German pastor martyred by the Nazis, labeled cheap grace: the perception that Christianity offers only a flood of blessings, the rights of the Kingdom without responsibilities to the King." Cheap grace! Religion without a price, without a cost, without the cross! You have to *pay the toll to reach the goal!*

Have you heard of the little boy protesting to his mother at the dinner table? "Why," he wanted to know, "are all the vitamins in spinach and not in ice cream where they ought to be?" Would you believe that there are adults who ask the same question? Why can't I be a Christian on my own, without all the hassles, without getting in with fellow believers in a church somewhere, without growing and learning and serving alongside them?

Why? Because Christ says we can't. "Whoever would save his life will lose it, and whoever would lose his life for My sake will find it." "If anyone desires to come after Me, let him deny himself and take up his cross, and follow Me." That's the way we move along with Him toward the Kingdom. We pay the toll to reach the goal, and that is true of everything worthwhile in life!

But now, having said all that, there is one glaring exception. There is one toll you cannot pay. It's already been paid. It's been paid by the only One who had the wherewithal to pay it! *It's the toll through heaven's gate.* It's the toll of redemption and salvation and atonement. It's the toll by which we get totally right with God. It's the toll Jesus paid on Calvary when He died on the Cross. It's the toll without which there is no Resurrection and without which the New Testament teaches there is no Eternal Life. He came for this express purpose, and He acknowledged it on the Cross when at the end He declared, "It is finished!" (John 19:30.) The debt had now been paid. Our moral and spiritual insolvency had been dealt with, graciously absorbed into the sacrificial love of the divine economy of God!

> We may not know, we cannot tell,
>   What pains He had to bear;
> But we believe it was for us
>   He hung and suffered there.
>   From *A Diary of Private Prayer*
>   by JOHN BAILLIE

So there is nothing more you or I can do about that. It's all been done! He did it! All we can do and must do to receive the benefit of His sacrifice is identify with Him, claim Him as Lord, claim Him as Savior. "There is no other name under heaven given among men by which we must be saved" (Acts 4:12). We take up *our* cross, not His. We do *our* part, not His part. For in walking with Him, confessing Him before an unbelieving world, acknowledging Him in all ways, there is a price.

There is a price for loyalty. There is a price for being different. There is a price for breaking with the crowd, or the ordinary, or the average, or the complacent. There is a price for going for the big one or reaching for the best. There is a price for leaving the familiar, well-worn ways and traveling the High Way that leads to God. While there is no price we can pay for salvation, be sure of this: There is a price, a high price, for faithful discipleship! You have to *pay the toll to reach the goal!*

I am reminded of an old legend about Saint Martin of Tours. One day, as he was seated in his prison cell, there was a knock on the door. Suddenly an august presence entered. There was something momentous about this mysterious figure and Saint Martin was uncertain as to who his visitor might be. "Who are you?" he inquired.

"I am the Savior," came the answer. Saint Martin was not convinced.

"Where then are the prints of the nails?" he asked. Whereupon, so the story goes, the devil vanished!

Pay the toll to reach the goal!

SIXTEEN

ANGELS WATCHING OVER YOU!

WHAT ARE YOUR thoughts about angels? Have you seen any? Would you know one if you did? What would you expect? Did you know that angels may be watching over you right now?

Amy Grant is a sensational popular singer of contemporary Christian songs. She has one song that goes like this:

> Angels watching over me,
> Every move I make.
> Angels watching over me,
> Every step I take.

While you may not have heard the song sung by Amy Grant, I'm sure you're familiar with the words of the ninety-first Psalm. They have a spectacular message: "For He shall give His angels charge over you, to keep you in all your ways" (Psalms 91:11). Have you thought about that—that God's angels may be watching over you?

I tell you, I believe in them! I've had my experiences with them. I am alive today because of them. They are my guardian angels. But I think of them in the biblical sense, as the Bible teaches. It's important that we understand the biblical teachings, for the world doesn't put much stock in angels.

A few years ago, the nationally recognized and widely respected sociologist Peter Berger wrote a book called *A Rumor of Angels*. Dr. Berger said the modern world dismisses their reality too easily, but then the modern world has a secular mindset and has little interest in what we call, for want of a better term, the *supernatural*. But to this sociologist the whole matter was up for review. There is, he said, this sense of the "Totally Other," of an awesome and overwhelming power which we should not ignore. So, therefore, a rumor of angels!

When the Bible speaks of angels, they are not quite the strange, fairylike figures we sometimes think. They are really quite human—in appearance, at least. They are certainly not at all spooky. They generally appear at the right moment, in the nick of time, when the need is greatest. Often they are simply messengers of God, or representatives, emissaries of God's love. Still, they are like people, or they are, in fact, people. The writer of Hebrews recommends that we treat all strangers with respect and courtesy because, he says, sometimes we "have unwittingly entertained angels" (Hebrews 13:2). It could be your angel who's watching over you!

Notice, too, how often in the life of Jesus angels appeared—at the most critical times, particularly at times of great decisions. At the beginning of His ministry when He withdrew into the wilderness and wrestled with the devil, we are told that "angels came and ministered to Him" (Matthew 4:11). Or again, on the eve of His trial and execution, when He prayed in the Garden of Gethsemane, we are told that "an angel appeared to Him from heaven, strengthening Him" (Luke 22:43).

Personally, I don't feel I can impose limits on the Almighty as to what He can or cannot do. There is, you see, something a little presumptuous about this modern age of ours and those who accept its thoughts and values. It's the spirit of the times to be quite sure, perhaps a little *too* sure, of ourselves, and quite certain as to what God may or may not do. We have forgotten His Word on this: "My thoughts are not your thoughts, nor are your ways My ways" (Isaiah 55:8).

What we need, you see, is a greater sense of the mystery and the wonder of God. A T-shirt I noticed the other day carried this intriguing message: "God is awesome." A pretty good message, I would say. Without that sense of His awesomeness, it is doubtful that when we think of God we are really dealing with God. It may be the fabrication of our own minds, perhaps, but not God. For "with God all things are possible" (Matthew 19:26), even angels.

We need a strong dose of agnosticism. We need to doubt and to question the glib assumptions of our age, because in the course of time and in the flow of history, most of the assumptions of an age prove to be false. Dean Inge, a very sharp man with an equally sharp tongue, once said that a man who marries the spirit of the age will soon find himself a widower! So, it may not be fashionable at the present moment to believe in angels, but I do. And I believe in your angels watching over you!

Let me tell you a remarkable story. It has to do with a dear and much-respected friend of many years, Dr. Charles Leonard Copenhaver. He was, in my judgment, one of the ablest ministers of our century. His gifts were extraordinary. His power in the pulpit was exceptional.

He served some of the great churches of our time, such as the four-thousand-member Reformed Church of Bronxville, New York. He was for many years the speaker over WNBC Radio's "Art of Living" series, an assignment he took over from Norman Vincent Peale. He was a prince of the pulpit, and he was also one of my dearest friends.

You see, I worked under Charles for three years while I was at graduate school in New York City, at Union Theological Seminary. It was an exceptional opportunity, and I have long believed the Lord had His hand in it. But thus began a lifelong friendship. We were frequently in touch for more than thirty years. Only a few weeks before his death we were together for lunch. I felt a strange urgency about our getting together when he called and suggested that we meet. Somehow I knew it was a date I must keep.

But let me tell you the most remarkable thing, something graciously shared with me by Charles's son, Martin, who a few years ago became the senior minister of the First Congregational Church of Burlington, Vermont. Shortly after beginning his ministry there, Martin was to have a weekend visit from his parents. Charles and Marion Copenhaver drove up from Connecticut, where they had moved a few months before upon Charles's retirement. They stopped for the night at the Hanover Inn in Hanover, New Hampshire. It was their plan to continue on to Burlington the next morning.

It was a Friday night, and they attended a concert or a play at Dartmouth, after which they returned to the inn. As they stepped off the elevator at their floor, Charles suddenly felt gravely ill. He gave Marion their room key and asked her to hurry ahead to open the door. Within seconds, Charles fell to the floor and was unconscious. He was having what proved to be a fatal heart attack. There was Marion, alone, in that hallway, while her husband

and companion of many years was dying. She called out for help to somebody on the elevator and asked that an ambulance be summoned.

At that moment, a woman appeared in the doorway of a nearby room. She came forward and stood beside Marion and remained with her. She subsequently accompanied Marion to the hospital, this total stranger who had stepped out of nowhere.

"I don't even know your name," said Marion, as they rode together to the hospital, whereupon they both introduced themselves. Hearing the name "Copenhaver," the woman asked, "Are you any relation to Charles Copenhaver?"

"Why, yes," responded Marion. "He is my husband. He is the one who was just taken to the hospital."

"Well," said the woman, registering astonishment at the coincidence, "your husband and my husband are very good friends. I have heard your name many times."

It turned out that these two men belonged to the same honorary society in New York City and were often together. The woman indicated that she was on her way to meet her husband. She had left a day early to spend the night at Hanover, although she had never done this before because she was unaccustomed to traveling alone. This one time she had made an exception, and so it was that she was there, at that hotel, on that floor, in that room—right near the spot where Charles collapsed.

This woman of mercy remained with Marion for some time, until word came that Charles could not be revived and until Martin Copenhaver had arrived to assist his mother. Marion subsequently noted that she did not know what she would have done without that woman at that overwhelmingly critical time.

But that isn't the end of the story. A few days later,

when she returned home following the memorial service for Charles, Marion went into his study at home. There on top of his typewriter was a letter, the last letter he had ever written. Incredibly, it was addressed to the husband of the woman whose appearance had been so timely at the Hanover Inn. Charles had written regrets, telling his friend he would be unable to attend the next meeting of their society because of "a previous engagement."

Shortly thereafter, Marion was describing this unusual incident to Dr. Norman Vincent Peale, a friend of the Copenhavers for many years. "Isn't it strange?" she commented, as she concluded her story. "It isn't strange," replied Dr. Peale. "That woman was one of God's angels who was there to minister to you."

I believe in angels. Don't you? I believe in the power of God to do whatever He chooses, whenever He chooses, however He chooses. And I believe His angels are watching over you!

SEVENTEEN

BELIEVING IN MIRACLES IN A SCIENTIFIC WORLD

THERE'S A SONG on the airways about miracles. I don't know who sings the song. I don't know where it comes from. I don't know how to classify it. But I do know its message: "Miracles, miracles, that's what life's about."

It's hard to think of faith without miracles. We are forever celebrating them—the miracles of Jesus. There's the miracle of His birth. There's the miracle of His life, the miracle of His ministry, the miracle of His Resurrection, the miracle of His coming. There are the many miracles Jesus performed and the Apostles performed after Him. And there are the miracles of lives transformed by Jesus Christ! How could anyone not believe in miracles and claim to be a follower of Jesus?

We have a slogan for the First Church of Christ in Wethersfield. It is: "Where the Spirit Is Alive and Miracles Happen." Many in our congregation will testify to miracles in their lives, many of them associated with their coming into our church.

A woman who joined our church not long ago came to us for a miracle. A year before joining she needed a church. She had gone through major tragedies in her life. She was at her wits' end. She was desperate. She needed something, and maybe there was a church where she could find it. She consulted the yellow pages of the telephone book and saw our ad, and the slogan, "Where the Spirit Is Alive and Miracles Happen." She called the church. "Is this where miracles happen?" she asked. The person answering the phone responded, "Yes!" How glad I am that person didn't hedge, didn't try to qualify it, didn't pull back on faith. What would have happened to that woman if we had failed her then? But because we professed to be such a church, a church of the Spirit and of miracles, she decided to come, and she kept coming! She discovered it was true: Ours is a place "Where the Spirit Is Alive and Miracles Happen." A miracle happened in her life. She came out of her difficult time, became a new woman, and now she belongs to our church!

Of all the miracles attributed to Jesus, none is more stunning than that recorded in Luke 8:22–25. "Now it happened, on a certain day, that He got into a boat with His disciples. And . . . as they sailed He fell asleep. And a windstorm came down on the lake, and they were filling with water, and were in jeopardy. And they came to Him and awoke Him, saying, 'Master, Master, we are perishing!' Then He arose and rebuked the wind and the raging of the water. And they ceased, and there was a calm. But He said to them, 'Where is your faith?' And they were afraid, and marveled, saying to one another, 'Who can this be?' For He commands even the winds and water, and they obey Him!' "

Now, in the face of that, we could take the easy way out, couldn't we? We could come up with a nice, acceptable explanation and entirely dismiss the intention of the passage and deny that this was a miracle. Frankly, that would be a sell-out to the secular mentality of the times. Moreover, it would be intellectually dishonest. I believe we have to come to terms with the miraculous, certainly in this faith of ours, and that's why I've titled this chapter "Believing in Miracles in a Scientific World."

But first, what is a miracle? How might we define it? How might we understand it? This is critical. It is pivotal. The definition we come up with locks us in, and maybe into an ultimately inadequate and inferior conclusion or understanding. "Define your terms" is always a good start! So what is a miracle? Let me give you my definition:

A miracle is an event of such an extraordinary nature that one responds with awe, and with a sense of mystery and wonder and of the divine. It is often seen as a demonstration of divine intervention and of divine overpowering in the normal course of events.

Now, that's our definition of a miracle, and having stated it, let's go on to make four fundamental statements about miracles: First, it is impossible to think of the Christian faith without miracles. Second, it is impossible to understand modern science in its true nature without an acknowledgment of the possibility of miracles. Third, it is impossible to look at life and see it whole without a sense of miracles. And fourth, it is impossible to believe in God without believing in miracles. Remember the song, "Miracles, miracles, that's what life's about"? Keep remembering it!

Now, let's look in detail at these points.

First, *it is impossible to think of the Christian faith without miracles.* Look at Jesus. Look at the New Testament. Look at the Gospels and the Book of Acts. Page after page after page report miracles that Jesus performed, miracles of every character. Not only did He perform them, He stated they were signs of who He was and what was going on!

In the seventh chapter of Luke, the disciples of John the Baptist come to Him and ask, on behalf of John, "Are You the Coming One, or do we look for another?" The text immediately cites miracles: "And that very hour He cured many people of their infirmities, afflictions, and evil spirits; and to many who were blind He gave sight." Jesus said to the disciples of John, "Go and tell John the things you have seen and heard" (Luke 7:19–22). These were signs. They were confirmations of His identity and of His mission.

Moreover, the whole history of the fantastic development and expansion of the early Church is based upon the theme of the miraculous. This is what caught the attention of people in the ancient world and compelled their response. This is a matter of historical record. Most of all, the concept of the Incarnation itself, that "the Word became flesh and dwelt among us . . . full of grace and truth" (John 1:14), is the central miracle of our faith.

So, however disconcerting it may be, however upsetting to the pet assumptions of our age, however tempting on the basis of some superior understanding that we suppose we possess, it is impossible to think of the Christian faith without miracles! That is fact Number One!

Second, *it is impossible to understand modern science, in its true nature, without an acknowledgment of miracles.* Now, we rightly celebrate the accomplishments of modern science. We are grateful for them. We can even speak of the miracles of science. It is a marvelous tool for knowledge and human progress. It is one way of acknowledging the glories of creation. Many of the best scientists marvel at the wonders of creation and of God's handiwork.

But having said that, we must understand that science is nonetheless a limited tool. Not only is it limited, it begins by making assumptions which cannot be demonstrated nor proved. These assumptions are of the nature of faith. So a true scientist is a person of faith.

What is that faith? What are those assumptions? First, this is a real world which we are studying or observing, something that actually exists. We cannot prove it. It could be a dream. The reality of the world, which we take for granted, cannot be proven. It can only be assumed. That's faith.

Second, this world can be known by the senses. In other words, we human beings, creatures of the earth, possess reliable equipment for knowing the world. That, too, cannot be proven. That, too, is an assumption. I suppose my dog is quite sure he knows what's going on, and in some respects he's better equipped. Certainly, his sense of smell is more acute, more reliable. But we assume our human senses are sufficient. Such an assumption is of the order of faith, not fact. Further, it limits us to knowledge of the natural realm while disregarding whatever there is of the supernatural realm.

Now, that means that science necessarily filters out any reality it cannot deal with. It pretends such does not exist. It does this only because whatever else there is is inconvenient for the assumptions of science and the method of science. That, of course, simplifies the process, but it may be absolutely wrong.

Certainly, science eliminates from consideration whatever is truly unique. It deals solely with what happens more than once, with what can be observed many times. This it calls the "normal." That is, whatever fits the norm. It deals with the repetitious and the repeatable; those events which, by the nature of things, occur again and again—like the sun coming up—and those events which can be repeated in a laboratory setting—like putting H_2O together again and again and each time getting water. Thus, on the basis of many such observations of things happening many times, science reaches conclusions about what is "normal." Note, however—and this is critical—it leaves out of consideration anything that does not lend itself to this method. It assumes for its convenience that the unique, the one-and-only, the non-repeatable, and the non-repetitious do not exist.

Are you familiar with halftones? These are photographic negatives prepared for the printing of a picture. If you look very closely under a magnifying glass at a picture made in this manner, you will discover the picture is not solid at all. It looks as though it were, but it is not. It really consists of tiny dots. It is not a complete picture. It merely looks as though it were. The real image has been screened out, leaving an *impression* of reality.

Now, that's what science does. It screens out a lot of reality. It gives an impression of completeness but without completeness. So our scientific perception is, to some extent, an illusion. It's not the whole story! By definition, it leaves out much of reality and most certainly the supernatural. That's why we say it's impossible to understand modern science in its true nature without an acknowledgment of the possibility of miracles.

Third, *it is impossible to look at life without a sense of miracles.* Many things happen to people where they must say, "It was a miracle!" When a child is born, at the very least, and if it is your child, and the full force of the mystery of birth is felt, you will say and believe, "This birth is a miracle!" Something wonderful may come into somebody's life, wholly unaccountable, and that person says, "I don't know how to explain it—it's a miracle!" Or somebody may go through a personal transformation— whether physical or mental, psychological or spiritual— and that person, or others, will say, "It's a miracle!" And unless you are of a cynical nature or equipped with an exclusively left-sided brain, you have said it, too. Everybody has! "Miracles, miracles, that's what life's about." Remember?

And fourth, *it is impossible to believe in God without miracles.* Let me qualify that: It is impossible to believe in *the God of Scripture*—the God who made the universe, the God who created the ends of the earth, the God who created the microcosm and the macrocosm, the God who knows the natural and the supernatural. It is impossible to believe in *this* God without an openness to the miraculous. For who would be so arrogant as to place limits on the divine? If your God is great enough to be God as Scripture portrays Him, then there is nothing He cannot do!

This is not to say He defies His own laws, even His natural laws. But it is to say He can apply *overriding principles and laws*. This is a concept advanced by the world-famous astronomer Harlow Shapley of Harvard. We say, he once noted, that water cannot go uphill. That is "normally" true. However if you lower a blotter on a spot of water or ink, you will see water or ink actually go uphill.

Some other principle, some other law, has taken over, taken precedence. There is no limit to the overriding principles or laws that can become operative in God's universe.

So, throughout creation and *beyond* creation, throughout the natural and *beyond* the natural and into the supernatural, the God who created all, who is above all and beyond all and in all, possesses the ultimate power to do whatever He chooses to do, if He is God! "With God, all things are possible," said Jesus (Matthew 19:26). Not all things are good, not all things are desirable, not all things fit His ultimate plan, but "all things are possible," because He is God!

Open your mind to this truth to know the power of God at work in your life. Open your mind to this truth to know the amazing and truly miraculous workings of God in and beyond creation. Miracles can and do happen. They happen all the time. "Miracles, miracles, that's what life's about!"

EIGHTEEN

ON BEING
FIT TO LIVE

WHAT'S GOING ON in your neighborhood? Let me tell you what's going on in mine. One day I had an early morning breakfast appointment at a nearby restaurant. I took the more scenic route from my house to the restaurant, by what is called Broad Street Green. Along the way, I passed several early-morning joggers. They were of all shapes and forms. One of them was a young woman wearing a grey sweatsuit. She was even wired for sound! She was wearing one of those cassette recorders with earphones so as she ran, she could listen to her favorite music. Now, how's that for sophisticated fitness!

People are literally running everywhere. They run up and down Main Street. They run by our church. Sometimes they run *in* the church! They run through the downtown park in the city during the noon hour. Some never stop. I heard of a man who got so carried away that, returning home, he ran straight through his screen door and "strained" himself!

No doubt about it, fitness has become *the* thing. People are really concerned about being physically fit. They want to be in shape. They want to be more vigorous and alive. And for good reason: They'll live longer. They'll accomplish more. They'll feel better. So there's nothing wrong with it and there's a great deal right with it. So here's our question: ***Are we really fit to live?***

You see, there's more to fitness than being physically fit. Real fitness encompasses all of life. It incorporates all of you—mind, body, and soul—not just a part of you. Exercise alone won't do it. Nutrition alone isn't sufficient. They're important, of course. I'm for all of them; that's my point! Good nutrition can ward off disease. Poor nutrition invites it. Did you know school children who eat a high protein breakfast do better in reading? Yet there is more to fitness than physical exercise or diet. A book called *Quantum Fitness,* by Irving Dardik and Denis Waitley, a doctor and a psychologist who have worked with Olympic athletes, points out that fitness includes exercise, nutrition, and the mind! Only a combination of all three, this book asserts, can give you "quantum fitness"!

Now, that's good! That's right! But I think we should take this one step further. There's a fourth aspect to fitness—the spiritual! We need the right spirit, or we need a fit spirit. The psalmist might have said, "Renew a *fit* spirit within me." You and I need soul-power going for us if we're going to be fit, totally fit—to live! Get that dimension into your total fitness program and you'll really have something going for you! Here's where the words of Hebrews hit home: "Therefore . . . let us run with endurance the race that is set before us, looking unto Jesus, the author and finisher of our faith . . ." (Hebrews 12:1, 2).

But, ***how do we do this?*** How do we become fit to live? What is the secret of total fitness that carries you all the way? There are five essential steps, it seems to me, for this kind of total fitness—the complete job!

First of all, you need to *get the right picture.* Picture the person you want to be. This visualization technique is now recognized as exceedingly important. You need to visualize the self you aim to become, the self you *can* become. You have to take time for this. You have to get and keep things in focus. If you want to lose weight, you have to look at yourself in the mirror and see yourself as you are, but equally you have to look at yourself through your mind's eye and see the self you want to become. To paraphrase Robert Schuller, "The me you see is the me you will be." Focus on that! "Psych" yourself with that. Says psychologist Denis Waitley: "Winners see the act of winning before it ever happens. . . . What you see in your mind's eye is what you get!"

Returning from a speaking engagement in Minneapolis not long ago, I flew to Chicago and then on to New England. At Chicago, a young man came aboard at the last minute. Quickly and energetically he strode down the aisle and took the window seat beside me. I noticed he had a remarkable build. His legs were massive—not fat, but apparently extraordinarily muscular. I concluded this was someone of enormous physical strength and power who must be into some special kind of program. "Who is this?" I wondered. "What's his line of work? Why is he in such great shape?" My curiosity was getting the best of me.

In a few minutes, we struck up a conversation. I learned that he was returning from the Olympics in Los Angeles. Now I began to understand! He was not a participant, not this time, but an official. At a previous time, he acknowledged, he had been a participant in the Olympics. It turns out his sport was fencing. Then I knew why this incredible build! Since ours was a give-and-take conversation, I told him I was in the ministry. I volunteered the thought that my job was like that of a coach: I helped people to get in shape for life.

Then I got into something I wanted to ask him about. What was there in this "imagining" technique? I had heard athletes were using it. Was there anything to it? He replied, "Oh, yes!" He went on to say that it was a very important part of the science of being a top athlete. Then he told me how that previous week he had seen athletes visualizing all the moves necessary to accomplish their feats—*before* they made those moves. This, he told me, really gives them a winning edge. That fascinated me, and it convinced me of something.

It convinced me that to become fit in any sense, you have to get the right mental picture. You have to *see* yourself as you want to be. You have to "psych" yourself with that self-image. Who is the person you'll feel good about, you'll feel right about, you'll be happy with? Spend time with that visualization technique even as Olympic athletes spend time visualizing their every move before they make them! For physical, mental, and spiritual fitness, get the right picture! Zap yourself with it! That's the first step!

The next step is, **get the right nutrients!** Get the right ingredients into your system. Feed yourself the right way to accomplish your purpose. Nutrition is important, no doubt about it—nutrition in all forms! What are the things we need to absorb to maximize the possibility of our becoming what we want to become physically, mentally, and spiritually? This means take charge of your intake. It means asking yourself what you are feeding on day after day. What are you taking in? In the computer field, the saying is "Garbage in, garbage out." In other words, get the right nutrients!

The lilac bushes beside my Vermont farmhouse weren't doing very well. You'd never have known I had planted them at least a decade earlier. Year after year, they stayed the same: No growth! No blossoms! I was disappointed. I felt like pulling them up. Then I faced the situation. What those bushes needed was fertilizer. The soil wasn't providing the necessary nutrients. From almost the day (stretching it a bit, but you get the point) that I put fertilizer into the soil around them, they grew. They came alive! Today, they are much, much bigger. They look great. And, yes, they have finally blossomed!

Lots of teenagers need to be reminded that fast foods won't do it. These kids can't grow, develop, and become the strong, tall, handsome or beautiful persons they want to be on fast foods. They need better nutrition. But the same is true for all of us, teenagers and adults, and the principle applies in all three areas of life—the physical, the mental, and the spiritual. Feed on junk and you get junk. Garbage in, garbage out.

Jesus was making this very point when He said, "Man shall not live by bread alone, but by every word that proceeds from the mouth of God" (Matthew 4:4). You see, fitness requires good nutrition, and spiritual fitness requires the nutrition of God's Word, God's Reality, and God's People. Get the right nutrition to fulfill your own wonderful self-image. Get the right nutrients to make it all happen!

The third step is, **get those workouts!** We can't get in shape and stay in shape physically without regular exercise. We have to walk. We have to run. We have to get active, get physical, and keep at it. This needs to be done regularly, not spasmodically. That means every day, every week. This isn't to say we won't resist at times. That's normal. That's human. Somebody said, "Whenever I feel the impulse to exercise, I sit down until it wears off!"

Ah, but what better results we get when we take charge of ourselves, take charge of our bodies and put them through their paces. It pays off! In no time, we're feeling better. In no time, we know it's worth the effort. My twenty-year-old son lifts weights and does a few other things to get in shape. I must admit, he looks terrific!

Recent studies of the mind show the importance of mental exercise. The mind responds to use much the same way as muscles respond to use. It also atrophies when not used. I read the other day that new research indicates the brain has its maximum connections and currents (not the technical terms, but they'll do) in the mid-teens. Then it shuts down, closes down, eliminates whatever it finds we're not using! Later in life, too, mental activity is a key to keeping mentally alert. It looks as though, barring illness or disease, the normal mind can keep developing well up into the seventies and eighties. Here, too, the key is: "Use it or lose it!"

But, if all of this is true of the physical and the mental, can anyone in his right mind believe the spiritual life is less demanding? Can anyone believe we can be spiritually fit without regular spiritual exercise? Jesus never thought so! He was adamant about this: If you wanted to walk with Him, you had to get up and get going! "Take up your bed and walk!" was His command. To those not inclined to take Him at His word, He had a stronger message: "Let the dead bury the dead." "Use it or lose it," He seemed to say.

Discipline in the spiritual life is as important as it is anywhere else if you're going to get in shape, if you're going to get fit to live with Him. You know what this means? It means daily spiritual exercise through prayer and the thoughtful, receptive reading of God's Word. It also means the spiritual exercise of worship with other believers in God's House once a week. That's it! No less! If we're going to be fit, we cannot delude ourselves, whether we're talking about physical fitness, mental fitness, or spiritual fitness. We need that workout, and when we've had it, we feel great! We really feel good!

Here's the fourth step: *Get in with the right crowd!* Boy, this is really important! People trying to get into shape, physically, find they need to get with others interested in the same thing—so they join a health club, or they go to the Y, or they collect jogging partners. Whenever anyone gets intentional about something, he or she generally looks for challenging and reinforcing associations pointed in the same direction. It's been this way for years, for centuries. We need the stimulation and we need this sharing of know-how—how to deal with this or that problem, how to handle this or that situation. It becomes a science, and then we really get good at it. People may think they don't need others, but it's an illusion they choose to live with. Be sure of this: They'll not be among the top performers! There's scant chance they'll be among any performers worth noticing!

Without close identification with the right crowd, we get badly influenced by the wrong crowd, the people who don't care or don't know. The vacuum gets filled, one way or another, with the right stuff or with the wrong stuff. Peer pressure is strong. The wrong crowd pulls people down. It gets them into things they wouldn't get into otherwise, and often, afterwards, they're sorry. They see what it's done.

Jesus made much of the importance of standing your ground against the counter-influences. Otherwise, He said, you can't make it in the Kingdom. The way He put it was, paraphrasing and summarizing Luke 12:49–53, "Anyone who would follow Me will be at variance with other people, even those closest to him; anyone who would follow Me will have to buck the crowd."

How many young people are selling themselves short because they've gotten in with the wrong crowd? The presure of their friends leads them into drugs, alcohol, and miserable, messed-up lives—from which, in many instances, they never recover. It's true, "You are the company you keep!" You become like those with whom you associate. There is "guilt by association," or at least *through* association. That's why it's so difficult, if not impossible, to be a Christian without the Church, without joining with fellow believers who are committed to Jesus Christ!

It was a long time ago, but I'll never forget a statement made to my father when, as a young man, he was in "the bike game." He had become a professional cyclist, and his mentor, "Major" Taylor, the man I consider to be the first great black athlete, was then the world's champion. He tutored my father in all aspects of the sport, and counseled him as father to son. He urged my father always to work out with those better than he, a class or notch higher. Then, of course, every race would be easier, since he would be prepared for superior competition. "Morgan," said Major to my father one day, "you have to race with the best if you want to be a champion!"

He was right, of course, in all ways. You have to get with the right crowd, run with the right crowd, race with the right crowd. That's why John Wesley, rejecting the individualistic, Lone-Ranger-type Christianity, pointed out, "The Bible knows nothing of solitary religion." It's a group experience, with the right group.

And the fifth step is this: *Get with the right Leader!* Who has ever attained excellence who has not had a model, a pacer, a coach, or a captain—someone who sets the pace? Every great artist had a teacher, an inspiration. Every great musician had a coach. Every great team has a captain. It's the final requirement of fitness: Turn yourself over to someone who knows more about it than you do, the expert, and learn from him.

We, in the Christian faith, have such a One. We have a Coach! We have a Leader! We have a Lord! Who else but Jesus Christ? That's why authentic Christianity is first, last, and always relational. It is built upon a relationship, a personal relationship, with Jesus! "Come unto Me," He says to each and all. "I am the way, the truth, and the life. No one comes to the Father except through Me" (John 14:6). Quite clear! Quite succinct! We need a Coach, a Leader, a Lord! And, believe me, we've really got One! He's my Coach! I hope He's yours!

Don Miller, football coach at Trinity College in Hartford and faithful member of my congregation, knows something about the need of a coach. He's one of the best himself. The *Hartford Courant* called Don "a credit to Trinity." He knows every team needs a coach. He knows a good team listens to the coach, keeps close to the coach, follows the coach. Anyone who knows anything about peak performers knows you need a coach.

Tom Landry, coach of the Dallas Cowboys and outspoken Christian, knows what he hopes they'll say about him: "The coach was right!" That's all he wants as the final judgment on his career and life. You can't prove it at the time. It's always a matter of faith and a matter of trust with a coach. You have to believe he knows what he's doing. If you can't risk it with the coach, you can't risk it with the team. You can hardly play the game! Only later will you know whether the coach was right!

Only later will *we* know our Coach, the Lord Jesus, was right! When the commitment is complete, when the lifetime of love and loyalty is sealed in a final and gloriously fulfilling moment and we meet Him face-to-face, only then will we know "the Coach was right!" But for the spiritual fitness we earnestly desire, as in any kind of fitness, we need the Leader, we need the Coach!

You want to be fit to live? The essentials are clear, and you can do it. You can take those steps. You can make the grade. So why not? Why not go for it? Get fit to live! Hebrews 12:1, 2 sums it up: "Therefore . . . let us lay aside every weight, and the sin which so easily ensnares us, and let us run with endurance the race that is set before us, looking unto Jesus, the author and finisher of our faith. . . ." The Leader! The Coach!

NINETEEN

THE SERENITY
OF ACCEPTANCE

WE'RE COMING DOWN to the wire. In these final chapters we're going to look at the most popular prayer in the world today. What is that prayer? I wonder whether you can guess, but let me qualify the question. Apart from the Lord's Prayer and maybe the Prayer of Saint Francis of Assisi, what would you say is the most universally loved prayer of our time? It's my opinion that it's the Serenity Prayer which appears literally everywhere—on note paper, posters, key chains, medallions, you name it. It's recited the world over. At every meeting of Alcoholics Anonymous, wherever and whenever that organization meets, it is part of the ritual of faith. Few prayers have become more familiar, few more beloved, than this:

> God grant me the serenity to accept the things I cannot change, courage to change the things I can, and wisdom to know the difference.

Why is that prayer so popular? Why do millions upon milliions respond to it? Why do innumerable people cling to it, reaffirm it, recite it, and surround themselves with its constant reminder? Isn't it that in those simple lines they recognize three key and all-important concepts for getting it together, especially if and when your world has come apart? Notice what it brings into sharp focus.

First of all, real serenity comes only through an attitude of acceptance. Evade that fact if you will, but that's the way it is. Second, if our lives are to move ahead and our future is to be bright and hopeful, we need courage to make critical changes here and now. Are we afraid of change, unwilling to change, annoyed by change? Maybe so, but the better refrain is, "There'll be some changes made!" And third, all of us, if we're to be successful in our efforts, need wisdom to make right decisions which will affect us profoundly and even eternally. We are decision-making creatures, we human beings, and by so many specific decisions we shape our lives, we fashion our destinies, for good or ill. No consideration of how to get it together when your world is coming apart would be adequate or certainly complete without coming to terms with these three truths exquisitely incorporated in the Serenity Prayer. They provide the inevitable culmination of our wrestling with issues of life and faith and God.

But first, a personal word. Let me tell you I view that prayer every day. A copy of the Serenity Prayer hangs in the family room of our home. It dominates the most frequently used area of our household. Beautifully embroidered, thoughtfully framed, it's the cherished gift of a friend and former parishioner. A certain woman who belonged to a church I once served loved the prayer enough and cared for us enough to take many long hours fashioning this gift that has graced our home for at least a decade.

There is another personal and treasured connection here. The Serenity Prayer is attributed to Dr. Reinhold Niebuhr, widely regarded as the foremost American theologian of our century. Dr. Niebuhr, I am proud to say, was my teacher at Union Theological Seminary when I was studying for the ministry in the early fifties. The prayer fits him, and I think of him whenever I say or hear it. There has been, more recently, the suggestion that perhaps Niebuhr did not write it himself. However, it seems evident he thought he did, and, frankly, I think he did. To me it reflects the spirit of my great and beloved teacher.

Let's focus on the first line of the Serenity Prayer, that part which deals with serenity and how it is found *through acceptance.* Is there anything more important than that? Have you learned "to accept the things I cannot change"? Or is that still a problem for you? Believe me, it's basic! Master this if you're really going to move ahead, if you're really going to enjoy peace of mind!

Think of how we make ourselves miserable. We do it by not accepting the inevitables of life! We keep fighting them! We keep thinking we can change them, overcome them, or set them aside when we can't. We simply do not settle it in our minds that there are some things over which we have no control and never will! The best thing we can do is to dismiss them, resolutely, from our range of concerns; put them out of our minds forever!

I am reminded of a frustrated father who was often annoyed by his teenage daughter's long conversations on the telephone. One day she got off sooner than usual, much to his surprise. "What happened?" he asked. "Usually you talk on the phone for two hours, but tonight you only talked for forty-five minutes! Why so short?" "I had a wrong number!" she answered.

So you want to make yourself miserable? Let me tell you

how. Refuse to accept the things you cannot change. Do you want to waste your life wallowing in self-pity? Let me tell you how. Refuse to accept the things you cannot change. Do you want to reduce your effectiveness, lower your vitality, diminish your elan, wipe away all chance for real success? Let me tell you how: Refuse to accept the things you cannot change. Do you want to risk driving yourself to drink or drugs, depression, and even death? Okay! Let me tell you how: Refuse to accept the things you cannot change!

This is one sure way to steadily but surely destroy yourself, drive yourself to an early grave. Have you heard this delightful little limerick?

A maiden at college, Miss Breeze,
Weighted down by B.A.s and Ph.D.s
    Collapsed from the strain,
    Said her doctor, "It's plain,
You're killing yourself—by degrees."[5]

Isn't that what we do? When we do not accept the things we cannot change, when we work ourselves into a state of distress, when we spend our energy needlessly, when we send poisons coursing through our veins into every part of our mind and body because of needless, useless, mindless frustration, we're killing ourselves "by degrees"!

What's the alternative? Simple! *Find serenity through acceptance!* Find peace of mind through acceptance. Find inner composure, inner emotional equilibrium through acceptance. Why, what a transformation can come through this prayer: "God grant me the serenity to accept the things I cannot change"! Well, then, what can you *not* change?

Here's one thing: **You can't change the past!** What's past is past. You can stew about it. You can cry about it. You can work yourself into a tizzy because of it. But you cannot change it!

You can't change the *distant* past, and you can't change the *immediate* past. You cannot change what happened long ago or what did not happen. You cannot change the loss you experienced, the sorrow you went through, the hardship you put up with it, the mistakes you made, or the deprivation you endured. You cannot bring back a bit of it. It's gone—forever! Nor can you change the immediate past, the dumb thing you did yesterday, the embarrassing slip of tongue a moment ago. That, too, is gone forever.

Several years ago one of my sons, then in his early teens, made one of the smartest statements I've ever heard. We were talking about some difficult things he had gone through, a transition he had made, and I asked him how he handled it so well. He looked at me and said, "Dad, you can't live in the past!" Wow! Out of the mouth of the young! Boy, was I proud of that son of mine!

Paul puts it gloriously, "Forgetting those things which are behind and reaching forward to those things which are ahead, I press toward the goal . . ." (Philippians 3:13, 14). That's it!

So, first of all, accept the past.

Here's the second thing you can't change: **You can't change your inheritance.** You can't change your background, where you came from, your beginnings. That's a given in life, so make the most of it; make the best of it.

One day I was having lunch with a very successful and fine-looking businessman. We were talking about some things troubling him. He admitted that for a long time he had been defensive of, if not embarrassed by, his ethnic background. I expressed surprise. I am not of that background, but I told him how much I admired it, what terrific things I saw going for him because of it. Yet for him it had been a matter of touchiness, sensitivity, even a little embarrassment. It had not brought out his best through the years that he had been unable to accept his heritage. Frankly, I talked to him like a Dutch Uncle. I tried to set him straight, or better yet, I tried to help him realize what a fantastic heritage he enjoyed.

So that's another thing you can't change and had better accept—your inheritance!

Here's the third thing you can't change: **You can't change the people around you.** They are who they are, and you are who you are. Yet how often we have the feeling we can change these people or that we should change them. We think, if only *they* would shape up, we could be happier and more contented.

Now, it's true—people around us do affect us. It would be great if they would be a little more to our liking or did not annoy us. And, if we think it might do some good, we can share with them gently, lovingly, and patiently our grievances. But better not depend for our happiness and peace of mind upon their coming around and shaping up and being exactly what we want. How many marriages get off to a poor start because one or the other of them thought he or she could change the other! It's a strategy doomed to failure, possibly dooming the marriage as well!

Too many people go through life blaming everyone else for their misery. It's like the child kicking the chair for getting in the way. "So-and-so made me do it," they may say. Or "So-and-so made me unhappy." No one makes us unhappy. Nobody makes us mad. We make ourselves unhappy, and we make ourselves mad. Oh, they may make it easier for us to have those unpleasant feelings and reactions, but, in the final analysis, the choice is ours. Happiness is a matter of personal decision!

"There are many antagonisms," said a dear friend and mentor of many years ago, Dr. James Gordon Gilkey, "which can be, should be, and *must* be quietly ignored." If you want serenity, if you want peace of mind, accept the people around you for what they are and expect that they probably won't change very much. Let them be who they are, even as they should let you be who you are. You can't change people!

Here's a fourth thing you can't change: *You can't change the nature of the world.* For the most part, the world will go on being what it is—a lot that is wonderful and beautiful, but also a lot that is ugly, cruel, evil, disturbing, and downright sinful. Now, of course, you can make a positive contribution. You can join hands with others in seeking human progress and amelioration. And, of course, it should trouble you that bad things, evil things, unjust things, go on in the world. But, in any event, don't allow your own inner state to be at the mercy of the state of the world.

We are followers of One who said, "In the world you will have tribulation" (John 16:33). He didn't say you *might*. He said you *will!* That's the kind of world we live in, a fallen world! If we live at the mercy of the morning news or the evening television, if we allow evil around us to invade and take control of our minds and create disturbance within, then we're in trouble! We have surrendered ourselves to the world and to the demonic.

So, as a faithful follower of Jesus, accept that the world,

for all its goodness and beauty, has a lot of ugliness and evil. Your peace of mind cannot, and must not, be dependent upon the state of the world! Jesus says, "In the world you will have tribulation." But then He says, "Be of good cheer, I have overcome the world." That's critical. That's the really important thing—be cheerful, in spite of it all! When you live in the mind of Christ Jesus, when you have this mind in you which was, and is, in Him, the discordant world cannot overcome you!

Here's the fifth thing you can't change: *You can't change who you are!* You can't change the person you essentially are. This goes beyond heritage and inheritance to what and where you are today. You have to learn to accept and to love yourself, to feel good about yourself, to have positive feelings about yourself. You have to thank God for creating you and making you the unique person you are. Because, while there is room for improvement, you are somebody already!

Do you know what is the largest church in the world? It's a half-million-member church in Seoul, Korea, of which Dr. Paul Yonggi Cho is pastor. Cho will go down in history as one of the great and significant spiritual leaders of our time. But earlier in his life, he wasn't satisfied with himself. He wanted to be somebody else. He wanted to be a Billy Graham or an Oral Roberts. He tried to imitate them, but the results were discouraging. He couldn't bring it off. He prayed, "God, I want to be like Billy Graham or like Oral Roberts. Please help me!" But then as he tells us, "the Holy Spirit spoke to my heart: 'My son, I need only one Billy Graham and one Oral Roberts in this world. I want you to be the one and only Paul Yonggi Cho.' "

Exactly! And I believe God wants you to be the one and only you. Begin by accepting yourself and knowing that

God accepts you just as you are. Sure, you've got pecu-
liarities, and maybe you'll shed them in time, or maybe
not. Sure, you've got some traits you wish were different,
some defects you wish were corrected, and some tendencies that you need to watch. The alcoholic must accept his
problem, who he is, and that the risk will always be there.
The compulsive gambler must understand that that com-
pulsion is always with him. But you have to start with
where you are, with who you are, and know that God
loves you and accepts you anyway, if you only turn yourself over to Him.

So thank God for yourself. Rejoice! Celebrate who you
are! You're somebody! God made you, and "God don't
make no trash." Say to yourself, "It's okay to be who I
am," and start from there.

Here's the sixth thing you can't change: *You can't
change the love and power of God!* That's constant. That's
steady. That's forever! Make your peace with that. Let the
love and the power of God flow freely and fully and powerfully through your life. Say to Him, "O Lord, I need
You! I invite You! I ask You to come into my life and take
charge. Run the show! You can make more of me than I
can make of myself. Help me to know I am loved, and that
in that love there is a power greater than all the powers of
the world, a power that never fails and never ceases to
be."

For, you see, the love and the power of God are forever.
They never change. "Jesus Christ is the same yesterday,
today, and *forever!*" (Hebrews 13:8, italics mine.) That's
for keeps. Accept it! Find serenity through the acceptance of this one thing you cannot change: the love and
power of God in Jesus Christ, our Lord and our eternal
Friend!

A story is told of a man who met a beggar. The man said, "God give you a good day, my friend."

"I thank God," said the beggar, "I never had a bad one."

"God give you a happy life, my friend," said the man.

"I thank God," answered the beggar, "I have never been unhappy."

"What do you mean?" asked the man.

"Well," said the beggar, "when it is fine, I thank God; when it rains, I thank God; when I have plenty, I thank God; when I am hungry, I thank God; and since God's will is my will, and whatever pleases Him pleases me, why should I say I am unhappy when I am not?"

The man looked at the beggar with astonishment, and said, "Who are you?"

"I am a king," he replied.

"Where is your kingdom?"

"In my heart," he answered quietly.

So begin here with this prayer: "God grant me the serenity to accept the things I cannot change."

TWENTY

THE COURAGE
TO CHANGE

IN THESE FINAL chapters we're looking at the three great roadblocks to life. We're looking at the three major obstacles to getting life together and moving ahead hopefully, confidently, and successfully. That's what the Serenity Prayer is all about. That's why the Serenity Prayer is powerfully appealing to so many. It really gets to people. It really deals with the central issues of your life and mine. Let's see what this means.

What are the *three roadblocks to life?* We've looked at the first: an unwillingness to let go of the things we cannot change. Now, in this chapter, we deal with the second major roadblock: failure to see where our efforts can really turn things around and then to muster the courage and find the power to tackle them. In the final chapter, we'll look at the third roadblock: the problem of living with indecision.

What I'm getting at is that there are often better answers, more helpful and effective answers, than we realize. Once we find them, we can do something about them. We can get moving. We can take off! But first we must find them.

Did you hear about the man who claimed he was "a light eater"? "You? A light eater?" said an unbelieving friend. "But man, you must weigh over two hundred pounds!"

"Two twenty, to be exact," said the man, cheerfully correcting his friend.

"Two twenty! How can you claim to be a light eater and weigh two hundred and twenty pounds?"

"Well," he said, "as soon as it's light, I start eating!"

There must be a better way! I'm convinced there is, and it lies in this beautiful, appealing prayer: *"God grant me the serenity to accept the things I cannot change, the courage to change the things I can, and the wisdom to know the difference."* So, now, let's look at the second important truth contained in Niebuhr's prayer, *the courage to change!*

Years ago I walked into a cobbler shop to pick up shoes I had left for repair the week before. I had stopped in a day or two previously, but the shoes weren't ready. Now I was back again, hoping they had finally been finished. When I asked for my shoes, the cobbler seemed embarrassed. He hesitated a moment, and then, with a look of sad desperation, he suddenly asked me: "Mr. Morgan, can a man get back?"

"What do you mean?" I responded.

The poor man proceeded to tell me he had been listening to me on the radio every morning. At the time I was doing a series of early morning devotional programs. He acknowledged he had been listening to me and that that morning he had decided that when I came in, he was going to pose his question.

"Can a man *change?*" he persisted. "Can a man *get back?*" I quickly sensed that his problem might be alcoholism and said, looking at him steadily but compassionately, "*Yes!* Absolutely!"

I do not know what happened to him later on. I do know I referred him to a member of Alcoholics Anonymous whom I knew. There was an effort to connect with this fellow. So far as I know, he got into A.A., made progress, and got on top of his problem. I am confident he "got back," as he put it. But it was critical that he knew and fully believed that change could happen, change was possible. With all the conviction at my command, I answered, "*Yes!* Absolutely!"

And it's true! I know it's true! I've seen many changed lives, marvelously changed lives, lives that have been miraculously transformed. Change, of course, is what faith is all about. "We shall all be changed," says Paul in 1 Corinthians 15:51. How deeply I believe that! Of course, in the context in which Paul was speaking, he referred to an ultimate change, but his statement applies to all of this wonderful life with Jesus! "We shall all be changed!" Boy, what a thrilling, hope-filling proclamation of faith that is! How desperately we need to believe it!

Did you know change is the name of the game in faith? We have different expressions for this, of course. "Growth in grace" is one. "Conversion" is another. "Born again" or "Born from above" is a third. Call it what you will, and at whatever stage, but the element of change is central to the Christian life. No doubt about it, whoever we are, whatever our circumstances, whatever our besetting sins, "we shall *all* be changed!" Thank God for that! Alleluia! Praise God! That means we dare to pray this prayer and to believe in the possibility of its fulfillment: *"God grant me . . . the courage to change the things I can."*

Where does that leave us? It leaves us in the realm of enormous, exciting, and life-changing possibility. A lot of things we cannot change; we've seen that. Some of us learn our lessons the hard way, after repeated and sometimes heartbreaking failure. We cannot change the past. What's past is past! We cannot change our inheritance. That is the "given" of our lives. We cannot change the people around us. Either we make the best of the situation, or we move on and associate with other people more to our liking. We cannot change the nature of this fallen world. There is much that is wonderful about it, but there is much that is sad, cruel, and evil—even demonic. Further, we are "in the world, but not of it." We cannot change who we essentially are. There is a uniqueness about ourselves that we had better accept. And we cannot change the love and power of God! That's where we want to conclude the things we cannot change, on that hopeful, ever-promising, all-conquering note.

Change, of course, is the nature of life itself. To live at all is to know change, to experience change. We have to accept that, too—things never stay the same. In New England we say, "If you don't like the weather, wait a moment. It'll change!" Life is like that—always changing. Sometimes we resist it. Sometimes we lament it. Sometimes we pretend it isn't happening, but, believe me, it is! Groucho Marx once questioned a woman on his television show. "How old are you, ma'am?" asked the comedian, never one to hold back on such matters.

"I'm approaching forty," she said, with a little reluctance.

"Approaching forty?" responded Groucho. "From which direction?" Yes, indeed, life is change! Accept that! Then capitalize on it! And remember Paul's beautiful words. "We shall all be changed!"

As we celebrate that, there is something we must acknowledge: **Change can be good.** Change can be our
friend. That is something we need to get straight in our
thinking. You see, many people don't like change. They
see it as an evil, as a threat. "I'm 100 percent in favor of
progress," said a man, reacting badly to the threats he
perceived around him. "It's all this change I'm against!" I
suppose, in all honesty, we all feel that way sometimes.
It's a human response. But then we need to stand back,
recover our perspective, and look at change for what it
is—usually our friend, not nearly so often our foe; our
ally, not necessarily our adversary; our hope for the future, not our threat in the future.

Change means vitality. Change means purification.
Change means creativity. Change means renewal. It's only
when things stand still, stay the same, that the opposite
sets in—the loss of vitality, the loss of purity, the loss of
creativity, the loss of aliveness! There is nothing more
important in life to understand than this. It's like a flowing
stream. You have to go with the flow, because flowing
water can be clear and pure and refreshing. Stop its flow
and it gets brackish and impure, full of sediment and
pollutants. What makes the Dead Sea "dead"? No flow!
There's no outlet, hence no change. The water stands still.
So it's called the Dead Sea. Life without change is dead.
Was that what Jesus meant when He said, "Let the dead
bury the dead"? It's a basic principle of life that to be alive,
to keep alive, to be vital, creative, and fulfilled, you have
to keep moving, keep active, keep changing, keep forging
ahead. Bruce Barton once said, "When you're through
changing, you're through."

What's true of individuals is true of a nation or a society
or a church. At the First Church of Christ in Wethersfield,
we're committed to change. We invite it! When you're

alive to the Spirit, you're in for change. To resist change may then be to resist the Spirit, to resist God. We are trying to be "the most wonderful church you can imagine," as one of our members glowingly put it. That's a large order. But it's possible. And it's our dream, our vision. Short of that, we invite decay, decline, eventual death.

One of the great philosophers of our time, Alfred North Whitehead, made this brilliant statement: "Advance or decadence are the only alternatives offered mankind." Let that sink in! What is it saying? Change is our friend, not our foe. "We shall all be changed," is the beautiful promise of Paul. In light of this fact, surely we can muster the "courage to change the things we can."

Now what can be changed? Where can we make our moves? What is amenable to our efforts? We've seen all the things we cannot change. Where are we left? We're left with **ourselves!** That's where we can make our moves. That's where great and exciting things can happen. For look at what you can do: You can change your attitudes toward things. You can change your relationships. You can change your reaction and response. And, in so doing, you can dramatically, gloriously change and improve yourself! You can become what Scripture calls "a new creation" in Christ (2 Corinthians 5:17).

First try this: **Change your attitude.** Turn it around. Shape it up. Get it into high gear. Make it positive and constructive. When you do that, you take the initiative. You take charge. You get the best *in* yourself and the best *beyond* yourself going for you. I came up with a saying sometime ago: "Change your attitude and lift your altitude." The "attitude" of the wings of a plane determines the altitude at which it can fly. It's the key to rising above things, moving up, climbing high, soaring far, and enjoying a most glorious view! George Bernard Shaw said, "You are the window through which you must see the world." Your attitude determines how you see things, and how you see things determines what you can do about them. So that's the first step: Change your attitude!

Here's the second: **Change your relationships.** How you relate to things is your own doing. It's your decision. Maybe you need to get some distance on those relationships. Maybe you need to end them altogether, and there are some for whom that's the best advice anyone can give. End them! Or maybe you merely need to renegotiate those relationships, working out new understandings. Maybe you need to assert yourself a bit more, and let it be known you intend to live your own life, find your own way, hold your own values, plot your own course. Jesus warned us that those closest to us may be a hindrance to our finding the Kingdom. If we are to follow Him, we may need to let others know we're going a different route, marching to the beat of a different drummer. We've seen we can't change other people, but we *can* change our *relationship* to them. When that happens, a whole new and positive era can begin! Dare to change your relationships, and see how much better you feel!

Here's the third step that can make a world of difference: **Change your reactions.** Lots of things you cannot change. We've stressed that. But you can change your *reaction* to them. You can change how you respond. Sometimes, when people discover they can no longer manipulate or control us, it changes everything. Dr. Viktor Frankl was a famed Viennese psychoanalyst and the founder of Logotherapy. Many of his greatest insights came out of

World War II experiences, when he was in a concentration camp. He was deprived of everything that makes for human decency. People around him were brought to the lowest level of human degradation. They were made almost subhuman. But Frankl saw there was one thing his Nazi captors couldn't take from him: *his freedom to decide how he would react.* "Love your enemies," said Jesus (Matthew 5:44). He was right. Love is the greatest power on earth. It is the most positive response, the most positive reaction possible. So long as you love, you retain mastery over the situation. "Love your enemies," someone said. "It will drive them nuts!" Of course, because then they will know you are still in charge! It will keep them off balance, and you will still have the upper hand by the power of your loving response.

These are the changes you *can* make: You can change your attitude. That alone will produce wonders. You can change your relationships. Maybe they are in bad shape anyway and need some changing. Extract yourself from those, and you will go a long way toward the **new you!** And change your reactions. That's the final, central, pivotal, and most potent point of your freedom as a child of God!

But now—and this is the crux of it all—what is the single greatest key to making these needed changes in your life? What's the most important Force available to you for turning your life around? I have news for you, good news—*the Good News!* It's Christ! It's the power of Jesus Christ! He can change you and help you as nothing else and nobody else can. It's another way of saying there is a Higher Power that can help us, but here we identify and call that Power by name: *Jesus!* When the Lord Jesus comes into any life, that person becomes a "new creature," a new person! Try that. Let it happen. Try living, not by your own power, or under your own steam, but by the power of God in Jesus!

> I wish there were some wonderful place
>   In the Land of Beginning Again;
> Where all our mistakes and all our heartaches
>   And all of our poor selfish grief
> Could be dropped like a shabby old coat at the door,
>   And never put on again.
>
> LOUISE TARKINGTON

There is such a place—where you are *right now.* There is such a One who can help—*Jesus Christ!* Lots of things you cannot change. You can waste a lifetime trying to change them, but they won't budge. They won't yield! At the same time, lots of things you *can* change, and it's to your advantage to tackle them and not put off another day doing so. You can change your attitude. You can change your relationships. You can change your reaction. And you can do it all by the power of Jesus Christ set loose in your life! "I can do all things through Christ who strengthens me!" (Philippians 4:13.) You can leave "that shabby old coat at the door"—right now, today, this very moment—and never put it on again!

How? Simply get on your knees, and say, "Yes, Lord Jesus! I want to be different. I want to be a new creation in You. I know You can do it. You can make it happen. I want it to happen. *So come, Lord Jesus, be mine and let me be Yours—forever!"*

TWENTY-ONE

THE WISDOM
TO DECIDE

IT WAS A beautiful, lazy summer afternoon in Vermont. Two of my grandchildren, my youngest son, and I drove down to the general store at the foot of the mountain. There we participated in a familiar family ritual: each buying an item. Just one! It might be candy. It might be an ice-cream bar. Or it might be a bottle of soda pop. Each would decide for himself which it would be. The greater the number of children and grandchildren involved, the more complicated and time-consuming the ritual becomes. As I stood at the counter, having picked up a few items for myself, I waited for each person to make his decision. Finally, since things were dragging out a bit, I announced as the storekeeper, noting these proceedings, smiled, "It's all very simple: You simply *decide* which it's going to be—candy, ice cream, or soda pop."

That sums it up! Life is making decisions, and our lives are the sum total of the decisions we make. Failure to make decisions means the abdication of responsibility and the neglect of opportunity. Making unwise decisions means increasing the likelihood our lives will turn out badly. Making good decisions enhances our prospects and contributes enormously to effective, happy, and fulfilled living. Here, then, is the third major roadblock to life, the third great obstacle to overcome: the inability or unwillingness to make good and wise decisions and then to follow through. Here is where we need **wisdom to decide!** It's the third phase in the greatly loved Serenity Prayer. Slowly, thoughtfully, repeat the prayer to yourself. As you do, reflect on how far we have come in our faith-search and on what issue is before us now.

God grant me the serenity to accept the things I cannot change, the courage to change the things I can, and the wisdom to know the difference.

But, first, remember where this prayer came from. It came from Dr. Reinhold Niebuhr, America's foremost theologian of this century. Neibuhr died in 1971, but among his legacies was this extraordinarily popular prayer. I'm proud to say he was my teacher. I'm glad I got to know him personally as well as to bask in his stimulating, exciting thought. He was an incredible man, and I'm thrilled to note there's something of a Niebuhrian revival going on. We have a lot to learn, or relearn, from this towering Christian thinker.

It was my privilege to observe Dr. Niebuhr in a variety of settings and circumstances. I ate with him in the Refectory, the dining hall at Union Theological Seminary. He often took time to break bread with the students. I visited his apartment on Friday evenings, a major event back then, when the good professor invited students in for a mind-boggling time of discussion and reflection. An evening with Niebuhr was the best evening of all! The room was always electric. The man's mind was unfailingly impressive. His spirit was consistently spacious, vital, and contagious.

I remember welcoming Dr. Niebuhr back to the seminary and back home when he was released from the hospital in 1952. He had had a stroke. The seminary community had been deeply alarmed, no, *shocked*, by his sudden illness. It seemed impossible that the mighty man could be brought low. What if he did not make it, did not survive? What if we lost him? Those were dark days for us. But he was recovering, and now he was coming home.

It so happened that just at the moment I was crossing the intersection at Broadway and 122nd Street and had reached the sidewalk, a taxi pulled up beside me. I looked, and there was Dr. Niebuhr easing his way out of the cab. I rushed over to welcome and to assist him. "Dr. Niebuhr," I announced, "this is the most wonderful day for Union Seminary!" Truly it was! Thank God, Niebuhr was back!

Along with his massive theological mind, Reinhold Niebuhr had a pastoral heart. He never lost it! He was "The Pastor" to the end. How he gathered us, his little flock, in the dining hall, or the Social Hall, or wherever he could assemble us! How he welcomed and delighted in those gatherings in his apartment, as he regaled us with his far-reaching and faith-filled mind, this amazing man who could make mental leaps from one age to another or one continent to another with the skill and ease of a trapeze artist!

But among his pastoral legacies was this prayer. America's favorite, the Serenity Prayer. Through that prayer, the mark of Niebuhr is everywhere to be found: On the wall of our family room. At meetings of A.A. Everywhere! What a beautiful prayer it is! How simple, how direct, how

right on! Doesn't it touch your heart? Doesn't it say something to you? Niebuhr truly lived that prayer! The mighty
man brings us all to God in the lovely lines of the Serenity
Prayer!

One other thing about Niebuhr—I named my dog after
him! I have a standard poodle, and when I was naming
him, I was aware that the poodle is a German breed. My
dog needed a German name, but what? Then I recalled,
Dr. Niebuhr had a standard poodle. His was white; mine
is chocolate brown. I remembered Niebuhr strolling
through the seminary quadrangle with his white poodle.
"Why not name my dog after 'Reinie' (Niebuhr's nick-
name)? That's a German name," I thought. "Why, then,
I'll always have a noted theologian at my side for instant
advice!" Well, I liked the idea, and so my dog became the
proud possessor of the name of the redoubtable Niebuhr.
How's that for name-dropping?

But now, back to the prayer, and it's all-important third
petition: *"Grant me . . . the wisdom to know the difference."* That, to me, means wisdom to distinguish, to make
good judgments, to make critical decisions basic to life—
wisdom to decide! Have you got that? Do you want it?
Surely you see how it could contribute to your life, the
wisdom to decide!

Life, as we've seen, is filled with decisions. We are
called to make them all the time. A certain man claimed
that in his home he and his wife had divided the decision-making responsibilities. She made the little decisions;
he made the big ones. She decided where they would live,
what car they would buy, what college their kids would
attend. That freed him for the big ones: what to do about
the crisis in the Middle East, when to hold a Summit
Meeting, how to handle the national economy!

The prophet Joel speaks of "the valley of decision" (Joel

3:14). "Multitudes, multitudes in the valley of decision!" Isn't that true for you? I know it's true for me! "Multitudes" of us are in that valley, and the very course of our lives is determined by the decisions we make. God grant us the wisdom to make them well! We're all of us at one fork in the road or another, and which we choose is fraught with opportunity, indeed the making of a destiny!

A few mountain ridges north of my Vermont mountain house is the former home of America's gentle poet Robert Frost. Not far from Breadloaf and the summer campus of Middlebury College is where New England's bard lived. Frost caught the significance of decisions in his poem, "The Road Not Taken":

> Two roads diverged in a yellow wood,
> And sorry I could not travel both
> And be one traveler, long I stood
> And looked down one as far as I could
> To where it bent in the undergrowth;
> Then took the other. . . .
> Oh, I kept the first for another day!
> Yet knowing how way leads on to way,
> I doubted if I should ever come back.
> I shall be telling this with a sigh
> Somewhere ages and ages hence:
> Two roads diverged in a wood, and I—
> I took the one less traveled by,
> And that has made all the difference.

Life is a series of decisions. Life is a series of forks in the road. One decision leads to another. One decision opens up the possibility of another. Are they good decisions or are they destructive? Do they lead to higher ground or lower ground? Do they set us up for something better and happier and more fulfilling? Or do they set us up for eventual defeat, steady decline, and self-destruction? What do we need? We need wisdom to decide, wisdom as we make decisions, wisdom to make the **right** decisions!

Did you know making decisons is the essence of human freedom? It is at the heart of what it means to be a human being. Becoming mature means taking responsibility for yourself, making the necessary decisions that affect your life. It's part of the growing-up process. It's part of becoming a full-fledged human being created in the image of God.

A psychiatrist was addressing a high school youth fellowship in a church I once served. Suddenly he leveled with those kids, "What you are today may be largely what your parents and your home have made you. What you will be tomorrow will be what you decide." There it is again—the importance of making decisions! There's no escaping it!

One of the things that makes a totalitarian society intolerable is its denial of human freedom. People have less freedom to decide things that affect their lives. The decisions are made for them. Something in us rises up and cries out against it; something rises up to assert itself. It's like the two dogs that met in West Berlin. One was from the western sector of Berlin, and the other was from the eastern sector. "How do you like this decadent, capitalistic city?" asked the western dog, reputedly a dachshund. "So-so," ventured the borzoi. "What's wrong with it?" inquired the dachshund, sensing reservations in the eastern dog's response. "Well, in East Berlin I get meat that is soaked in the finest vodka. My doghouse has an electric heater in it. Once a week I see a cultural movie." The dachshund was impressed. "If that's the way it is in East Berlin, why do you come to West Berlin so often?" The borzoi twitched a little and replied, "Every so often I have this need to bark."[6]

To be a human being is to be free. To be free is to make decisions. By making decisions we determine the course and outcome of our lives. No wonder we need to pray, "O God, give us the wisdom to decide!"

Many a young person today faces potentially devastating decisions. Will I go along with the crowd? Will I experiment with alcohol and drugs, even though I may damage my mind, distort my personality, and tempt the possibility of an early demise? Will I go along and engage in illicit sex even at the risk of losing control of my life, cheapening myself, and imposing tragic, painful consequences on the lives of others? Young people need wisdom to decide because life will not protect them against wrong choices. Nor will shallow counselors afford much comfort when things turn sour! Life is too wonderful to be wasted!

All of us at any age face momentous decisions that may have unfortunate consequences. We cannot make them and expect to be excused from the results. It's the price of freedom. It's the price of God-endowed human freedom and the potentiality of human grandeur. "What is the purpose of life?" asks the Shorter Catechism. (Actually "What is the chief end of Man?") I like its magnificent answer: "To glorify God and to enjoy Him forever." Are we ready for that? Will we embrace the glorious and eternal possibilities inherent in life?

> To every man there openeth
> A high way and a low,
> And every man decideth
> The way his soul shall go.

O God, give us the wisdom to decide!

It's true! There are some things we cannot change, and there are some things we can. In that all-important area where we can, we need the wisdom to make decisions!

A young black by the name of Jesse Owens heard a visiting coach at his junior high school talk about the power of decisions. "You can pretty well become what you make up your mind to be," said the speaker. "God will help you."

Later, young Jesse went over to the speaker and said, "I've decided what I want to be—the fastest man in the world." The coach said to him, "That's a great dream, but there's one problem. Dreams have a way of floating high in the sky and drifting around like clouds. A dream never becomes a reality unless you have the courage to build a ladder to your dream."

The coach then told Jesse how to build that ladder to his dream. "You build one step at a time. The first rung is determination—a refusal to give up. The second is dedication. Then comes discipline, and the fourth rung is your attitude."

Jesse Owens got the message and made his decision. He began to build his ladder toward becoming "the fastest man in the world," and he succeeded. He didn't do it all at once. Nobody does! He did it rung by rung, step by step. It's the only way!

> By the yard, it is hard,
> By the inch, it's a cinch!

So how do we choose? Like this: We look ahead and ask some searching questions.

First, *where will this road lead?* A choice must be made. Which will it be?

> And sorry I could not travel both
> And be one traveler, long I stood
> And looked down one as far as I could
> To where it bent in the undergrowth. . . .

Look down that road as far as you can. Ask yourself, *Where will it lead? Where will it bring me out? Where will I be when I get where I'm going?*

Second, **how will you feel about it when you get there?** When you've committed your precious life, your precious time, your precious talent down that way, will you feel good about it? Will you feel right? Will you feel proud? Will you feel fulfilled? We need to think about these things; after all, we have to live with ourselves.

Third, **will it bring glory to God?** You're somebody. You were created in God's image for a divine purpose. "God don't make no trash," that's for sure! Will this route bring glory to God? We're not likely to cover this ground again. That's acknowledged in Frost's poem:

> Yet knowing how way leads on to way.
> I doubted if I should ever come back.

So, will it be a credit to God? Will it be a credit to our Lord? I don't know about you, but speaking for myself, I hope that "in that day in which there is no sunset and no dawning," I will hear Him say, "Well done, good and faithful servant."

Fourth, **will it be an inspiration to others?** Isn't that why we're here—to inspire others, to help them see what is good and beautiful and right? Isn't that what we secretly long to be—an inspiration to other people? Don't we really want others to look up to us, certainly not down on us? Isn't there something deeply wonderful and satisfying in knowing that this or that person found a better way because of us? And isn't that what Jesus meant when He said we are the salt of the earth and the light of the world?

And fifth, *will it require a step of faith?* Will you need God's help because you know you can't manage it alone? It's too much! It's too big! Will this choice at the fork in the road throw you back on resources far greater than your own, so that you will need other people and you will need God? That's real faith, you know! Is this decision so wonderful, so daring, so courageous that you will need God's help every step of the way? Then make that decision! Go that route! Go for the big one! "A man's reach should exceed his grasp, or what's a heaven for?" said Robert Browning in one of his most magnificent and tantalizing lines.

"The valley of decision"—we're all in it, for all of life is a "valley of decision." By so many choices, we shape our destiny. By so many decisions, we create our future. God grant us the wisdom to decide!

But, friend, **there is one decision that secures them all,** that empowers and sustains them all—the decision to go with Jesus Christ. There is strength in the song that says,

> I have decided to follow Jesus,
> I have decided to follow Jesus,
> I have decided to follow Jesus,
> No turning back!
> No turning back!

Who would want to turn back, having started up the road with Him? Who could want any other Companionship, any other Leader, or Fellow Traveler, or Friend?

> Jesus is all the world to me,
> My life, my joy, my all,
> He is my strength from day to day,
> Without Him I would fall.
> . . . .
> He is my Friend.

Have you made that decision to go with Christ? Be sure of this: It's the greatest decision you will ever make! It's the one decision that seals and secures all the rest! It's the one decision you can stake your life on! It's the one decision that can turn everything around! It's the one decision that will help you get it all together and keep it all together. Someone once said, "With Christ at the center, the circumference takes care of itself." This is the one decision for *keeping* it all together for eternity!

Why not do it? Why not have **the wisdom to decide—for *Jesus?*** Why not do it today?

ENDNOTES

1. Adapted from Dick Van Dyke, *Those Funny Kids* (New York: Doubleday, 1975), p. 21.

2. Adapted from *Leo Roston's Giant Book of Laughter* (Crown Publishers, 1985), p. 191, 192.

3. Ibid., p. 216.

4. Adapted from Dick Van Dyke, *Those Funny Kids* , p. 20.

5. *Leo Roston's Giant Book of Laughter*, p. 169.

6. Adapted from *Leo Roston's Giant Book of Laughter* , p. 110.